Critical praise for this book

'Colombia is the worst humanitarian
sources are deeply rooted in Colomb
the hegemonic power that are no less
institutions. This study provides a uniquely perceptive analysis of the tragic
interaction, and its far-reaching implications for understanding the past and
the evolving global order.' – *Noam Chomsky*

'US administrations keep finding new excuses for intervening in Latin
American affairs. Colombia is the most blatant example, as Doug Stokes'
trenchant account of the US's shifting agenda – from Cold War, to guerrillas, then the drug trade, and now the "war on terror" – so forcefully
shows. Whether called imperialism or technical assistance, the consistent
result is state terror and human suffering on a vast scale.' – *James Petras,
Professor of Sociology (retired), Binghamton University, New York*

'The two great turning-points of the last few years have been, or so we've
been told, the end of the Cold War and 9/11. Not so, argues Doug Stokes,
in this most challenging of volumes. Now, as before, the United States pur-
sues the same hegemonic project simply using different cover stories – first
communism, then drugs and now terrorism – to justify intervention in
Colombia. For those looking for reassurance, this is not the book; for those
seeking to peel back the layers of officialese and get to the heart of things,
this is a must read.' – *Professor Michael Cox, London School of Economics and
Editor of International Politics*

'This is a well-researched and impeccably documented exposé of US dupli-
city and intervention in Colombia. As Doug Stokes shows, Washington's
rhetoric has changed from containing communism to the war on drugs and
terrorism. But behind it all is the same cynical policy of terror and repression against the Colombian people, to prevent social change and maintain
control. This book fills a critical gap in the literature on Colombia and on
post-Cold War inter-American relations. It also has wider implications for
International Relations theory and for our understanding of transnational
conflict in this era of globalization.' – *William I. Robinson, Professor of Sociology, Global and International Studies, and Latin American and Iberian Studies,
University of California–Santa Barbara*

'America's Other War paints a very disturbing picture. Highlighting continuities in Washington's strategy that go back to the Cold War and show up
elsewhere in Latin America, Doug Stokes shows that there is depressingly
little "new" about the growing US involvement in Colombia's conflict.
With very thorough research and a highly readable narrative, America's
Other War goes beyond the liberal–conservative debate over Plan Colombia, the 'war on drugs' and the 'war on terror', reminding us of the central
role played by the often brutal pursuit of economic interests.' – *Adam
Isacson, Director of Programs, Center for International Policy, Washington*

About this book

With the end of the Cold War, Colombia has become the third largest recipient of US military aid in the world, and the largest by far in Latin America. This aid is said to be for a US-backed 'war on drugs'. After September 11th US policymakers have also claimed that Colombia has become the principal focus of US counter-terrorism efforts in Latin America. This book overturns these arguments and demonstrates that Washington has long-supported a pervasive campaign of Colombian state terror. The 'wars' on drugs and 'terror' are in fact the latest pretexts for this policy. US military aid and training for Colombia is designed to maintain the pro-US Colombian state and continues to destroy threats to US economic interests whilst preserving strategic access to sources of non-Middle Eastern oil.

Using extensive declassified documents, this book lifts the lid on US policy in Latin America both during and after the Cold War. It demonstrates that the so-called war on drugs and now the new 'war on terror' are actually part of a long-term Colombian 'war of state terror' that predates the end of the Cold War, with US policy contributing directly to the horrific human rights situation in Colombia today.

This book is essential reading for students and scholars of US foreign and security policy, US–Latin American relations, International Relations, policy advisers, non-governmental agencies and the layperson interested in US foreign policy, human rights and globalization.

About the author

Doug Stokes is a lecturer in International Politics at the Department of International Politics, University of Wales, Aberystwyth

DOUG STOKES

America's other war
Terrorizing Colombia

Zed Books
LONDON · NEW YORK

America's other war: terrorizing Colombia was first published by Zed Books Ltd, 7 Cynthia Street, London N1 9JF, UK and Room 40, 175 Fifth Avenue, New York, NY 1010, USA in 2005.

www.zedbooks.co.uk

Cover designed by Andrew Corbett
Set in Monotype Dante and Gill Sans Heavy by Ewan Smith, London
Printed and bound in Malta by Gutenberg Press Ltd

Distributed in the USA exclusively by Palgrave Macmillan, a division of St Martin's Press, LLC, 175 Fifth Avenue, New York, NY 1010

A catalogue record for this book is available from the British Library.
US CIP data are available from the Library of Congress.

ISBN 1 84277 546 4 cased
ISBN 1 84277 547 2 limp

Contents

Acknowledgements

There are a number of institutions and people whose input into this project has been invaluable. I would like to thank my parents, Rebecca Du Rietz, and Jim Copperthwaite. I would also like to thank a number of the academic and administrative staff at the University of Bristol's Politics Department including Richard Little, Terrell Carver, Judith Squires and Anne Jewell. Jutta Weldes read and commented extensively on this manuscript and her input into this project over the years has helped me enormously. I would also like to thank Susan Robertson, Roger Dale and Mario Novelli at Bristol's Education Department for their tremendous personal support and the stimulating discussions we often had. Mark Laffey also provided much needed advice and support.

The dedicated staff at the Center for International Policy in Washington made the research for this book much easier than it might have been. I have also benefited from the exchanges and analysis of the Center's Adam Isacson. The same can be said for Paul Wolf and the Media Awareness Project. A number of staff at Human Rights Watch and Amnesty International also helped in this project, as has their extensive documentation on the human rights conditions in Colombia's unfolding crisis. A number of other individuals have helped over the years, including Noam Chomsky, Garry Leach, Justin Podur, Peter Wilkin, Frank Smyth and Al Giordano. I would also like to thank the UK's Economic and Social Research Council, which funded me throughout the completion of this project. Most of all I would like to thank Eric Herring, who was a constant source of support and professional guidance throughout the writing of this book.

Glossary

ARI	Andean Regional Initiative
AUC	United Self-Defence Forces (Autodefensas Unidas de Colombia)
CI	Counter-insurgency
CNP	Colombian National Police
CONVIVIR	Special Vigilance and Private Security Services (Servicios de Vigilancia y Seguridad Privada)
CUT	United Confederation of Workers
DEA	Drug Enforcement Administration
DoD	Department of Defense
ELN	People's National Liberation Army (Ejército de Liberación Nacional)
FARC	Revolutionary Armed Forces of Colombia (Fuerzas Armadas Revolucionarios de Colombia)
FDI	Direct Foreign Investment
FMF	Foreign Military Financing
FTAA	Free Trade of the Americas Act
FTO	Foreign Terrorist Organization
IDB	Inter-American Development Bank
IFIs	International Financial Institutions
IMF	International Monetary Fund
INC	International Narcotics Control
IR	International Relations
JCET	Joint Command Exchange Training
Los PEPES	People Persecuted by Pablo Escobar (Perseguidos por Pablo Escobar)
MAS	Muerte a Secuestradores (Death to Kidnappers)
MTT	Mobile Training Teams
NAFTA	North American Free Trade Agreement
OPEC	Organization of Petroleum Exporting Countries
SOA	School of the Americas
TNCs	Transnational corporations
UNDCP	United Nations Drug Control Programme
UNDP	United Nations Development Programme
UP	Patriotic Union
US GAO	United States General Accounting Office
USTR	US Trade Representative

Foreword by Noam Chomsky

As I write, I have just received the most recent of the regular notices from the Jesuit-based human rights organization Justicia y Paz in Bogotà, directed by the courageous priest Father Javier Giraldo, one of Colombia's leading defenders of human rights, at great personal risk. This notice reports the assassination of an Afro-Colombian human rights activist, Yolanda Cerón Delgado, as she was leaving the pastoral social office near the police station. Justicia y Paz reports that it is a typical paramilitary operation, in association with the government security forces and police. Regrettably, the event is not remarkable.

A few weeks earlier there had been an unusual event: a rare concession of responsibility. The Colombian attorney general's office reported that the army had lied when it claimed that three dead union leaders were Marxist rebels killed in a firefight. They had, in fact, been assassinated by the army. Reporting the concession, the *New York Times* observes that 'Colombia is by far the world's most dangerous country for union members, with 94 killed last year and 47 slain by Aug. 25 this year', mostly killed 'by right-wing paramilitary leaders linked to rogue army units'. The term 'rogue' is interpretation, not description.

The worldwide total of murdered union leaders for 2003 was reported to be 123, three-quarters of them in Colombia. The proportions have been consistent for some time. Not only has Colombia been the most dangerous place for labour leaders anywhere in the world (in so far as statistics are available), but it has been more dangerous than the rest of the world combined. To take another year, on Human Rights Day, 10 December 2002, the International Confederation of Free Trade Unions issued its annual Survey of Trade Union Rights. It reported that by then over 150 trade unionists had been murdered in Colombia that year. The final figure for 2002, reported by the International Labor Organization in its 2003 annual survey, was 184 trade unionists assassinated in Colombia, 85 per cent of the total worldwide in 2002. The figures are similar in other recent years.

The assassinations are attributed primarily to paramilitary or security forces, a distinction with little apparent difference. Their connections are so close that Human Rights Watch refers to the paramilitaries as the 'Sixth Division' of the Colombian army, along with its official five Divisions. As Human Rights Watch, Amnesty International and other human rights organizations have documented, political murders in Colombia – of which assassinations of union activists constitute a small fraction – are carried out with almost complete impunity. They call for an end to impunity, and termination of US military aid as long as the atrocities continue with scarcely a tap on the wrist. The military aid continues to flow in abundance, with pretexts that are an embarrassment.

It remains to be seen whether the September 2004 concession of the army murders leads to any action. If the past is a guide, nothing will happen beyond the lowest levels, though the evidence for higher military and civilian responsibility is substantial.

There have been a few occasions when major massacres were seriously investigated. The most significant of these was the Trujillo massacre in 1990, when more than sixty people were murdered in a particularly brutal army operation, their bodies cut to pieces with chainsaws. Under the initiative of Justicia y Paz, the Samper government agreed to allow an independent commission of investigation, including government representatives, which published a report in shocking detail, identifying the military officer in charge, Major Alirio Urueña Jaramillo. Ten years later, Father Giraldo reported that nothing had been done: 'Not one of the guilty has been sanctioned,' he said, 'even though many more victims have come to light in subsequent years.' US military aid not only continued to flow, but was increased.

By the time of the Trujillo massacre, Colombia had the worst human rights record in the hemisphere – not because atrocities in Colombia had markedly increased, but because atrocities by El Salvador and other US clients had declined. Colombia became by far the leading recipient of US military aid and training, replacing El Salvador. By 1999, Colombia became the leading recipient of US military aid worldwide (excepting Israel–Egypt, a separate category always), replacing Turkey – not because atrocities in Colombia had increased, but because Turkish atrocities had declined. Through the 1990s, Turkey had conducted its brutal counter-insurgency war against its domestic Kurdish population, leading to tens of thousands of deaths and probably millions driven from their devastated villages, many surviving somehow in condemned buildings in miserable slums in Istanbul, in caves in the walls of the semi-official Kurdish capital of Diyarbakir, or wherever they can. The atrocities were accompanied by vicious torture, destruction of lands and forests, just about any barbaric crime imaginable. Arms from the USA came in an increasing flow, amounting to about 80 per cent of Turkey's arms. In the single year 1997, Clinton sent more arms to Turkey than the cumulative total for the entire Cold War period prior to the onset of the counter-insurgency campaign. But by 1999, the campaign had achieved 'success', and Colombia took over first place. It also retains its position as 'by far the biggest humanitarian catastrophe of the Western hemisphere', as UN Undersecretary for Humanitarian Affairs Jan Egeland reiterated at a press conference in New York in May 2004.

There is nothing particularly novel about the relation between atrocious human rights violations and US aid. On the contrary, it is a rather consistent correlation. The leading US academic specialist on human rights in Latin America, Lars Schoultz, found in a 1981 study that US aid 'has tended to flow disproportionately to Latin American governments which torture their citizens … to the hemisphere's relatively egregious violators of fundamental human rights'. That includes military aid, is independent of need, and runs through the Carter period. In another academic study, Latin Americanist Martha Huggins reviewed data for Latin America suggesting that 'the more foreign police aid given [by the USA], the more brutal and less democratic the police institutions and their governments become'. Economist Edward Herman found the same correlation between US military aid and state terror worldwide, but also carried out another study that gave a plausible explanation. US aid, he found, correlated closely with improvement in the climate for business operations, as one would expect. And in US dependencies it turns out with fair regularity, and for understandable reasons, that the climate for profitable investment and other business operations is improved by killing union activists, torture and murder of peasants, assassination of priests and human rights activists, and so on. There is, then, a secondary correlation between US aid and egregious human rights violations.

There have been no similar studies since, to my knowledge, presumably because the conclusions are too obvious to merit close inquiry.

The Latin American Catholic Church became a particular target when the bishops adopted the 'preferential option for the poor' in the 1960s and '70s, and priests, nuns and lay workers began to establish base communities where peasants read the Gospels and drew from their teachings lessons about elementary human rights, and worse yet, even began to organize to defend their rights. The horrendous Reagan decade, commemorated with reverence and awe in the United States, is remembered rather differently in the domains where his administration waged the 'war on terror' that it declared on coming to office in 1981: El Salvador, for example, where the decade is framed by the assassination in March

1980 of an archbishop who had become a 'voice for the voiceless' and the assassination of six leading Latin American intellectuals, Jesuit priests, in November 1989, by an elite force armed and trained by the USA which had left a shocking trail of blood and torture in earlier years. The (now renamed) School of the Americas, which has trained Latin American officers, including some of the continent's most outstanding torturers and mass murderers, takes pride in having helped to 'defeat liberation theology', one of the 'talking points' in its public relations efforts. Such matters arouse little interest in the West, and are scarcely known apart from specialists and the solidarity movements. The reaction would be somewhat different if anything remotely similar had taken place in those years in the domains of the official enemy.

The basic principles of state terror are explained by Schoultz in a standard scholarly work on US foreign policy and human rights in Latin America. Referring to the neo-Nazi 'national security states' imposed or backed by the USA from the 1960s, Schoultz observes that the goal of state terror was 'to destroy permanently a perceived threat to the existing structure of socioeconomic privilege by eliminating the political participation of the numerical majority ... [the] popular classes'. All of this is very much in accord with the basic principles of the counter-insurgency (CI) doctrines that have been core elements of US foreign policy since the Second World War, as Doug Stokes reviews, doctrines that remain quite consistent while pretexts change, as does their implementation, as again Stokes reviews in illuminating detail.

Colombia's rise to first place as a recipient of US military aid in 1999, replacing Turkey, was particularly striking at that particular moment. The transfer, which passed without notice in the mainstream, came right in the midst of a chorus of self-adulation among Western elites and praise for their leaders that may have been without historical precedent. Respected commentators gazed with awe on 'the idealistic New World bent on ending inhumanity' as it entered a 'noble phase' of its foreign policy with a 'saintly glow', acting from 'altruism' alone and following 'principles and values' in a sharp break from the past history of the world as it led the way to establishing a 'new norm of humanitarian intervention'. The jewel in the diadem, opening a new era of world history, was the bombing of Serbia in 1999. Whatever one thinks of the crimes attributed to Serbia in Kosovo prior to the bombing (which, as anticipated, led to a radical escalation of the crimes), they do not compare with the unnoticed actions of Western clients, not only the leading recipients of US military aid but others as well: East Timor, to take a striking example from those very months, while US–UK support continued as atrocities once again escalated well beyond anything reported at the time in Kosovo by official Western sources.

As is well-known, the 'drug war' provides the recent justification for support for the security forces and (indirectly) their paramilitary associates in Colombia. With the same justification, US-trained forces, and mercenaries from US corporations that employ ex-military officers, carry out 'fumigation', meaning chemical warfare operations that destroy crops and livestock and drive peasants from their devastated lands. Meanwhile the street price of drugs in the USA does not rise, implying that the effects on production are slight, and the prison population in the USA explodes to the highest recorded level in the world, far beyond other industrial societies, largely as a consequence of the 'drug war'. It has long been understood that the most effective way to deal with the drug problem – which is in the USA, not in Colombia – is education and treatment, and the least effective by far is out-of-country operations, such as chemical warfare to destroy crops and other CI operations. Funding is dramatically in inverse relation to effectiveness, and is unaffected by failure to achieve the claimed goals.

The facts, hard to miss, raise some obvious questions. One of the leading academic authorities on Colombia, Charles Bergquist, remarks that 'a provocative case can be made that US drug policy contributes effectively to the control of an ethnically distinct and economically deprived underclass at home and serves US economic and security interests abroad'. Many criminologists and international affairs analysts might regard this as a considerable understatement. Faith in the proclaimed doctrines becomes still harder to sustain when we attend to the relation between US resort to subversion and violence and increase in drug production back to the Second World War, documented in rich detail by Alfred McCoy, Peter Dale Scott and others, recurring right at this moment in Afghanistan. As Scott observes, reviewing many cases of US military intervention and subversion, with each 'there has been a dramatic boost to international drug-trafficking, including a rise in US drug consumption'. At the same time, the lives of Colombian campesinos, indigenous people and Afro-Colombians are destroyed with the solemn claim that it is imperative to carry out these crimes to prevent drug production and use.

In extenuation, it could be noted that fostering drug production is hardly a US innovation: the British empire relied crucially on the most extraordinary narco-trafficking enterprise in world history, with horrifying effects in China and in India, much of which was conquered in an effort to gain a monopoly on opium production.

The official pretexts are confronted with massive counter-evidence, and supported by no confirming evidence (apart from the declarations of leaders, which invariably speak of benign intent and are therefore uninformative, whatever their source). Suppose, nevertheless, that we accept official doctrine, and assume that the goal of the US-run CI operations in Colombia, including the chemical warfare that is ruining the peasant society, is to eradicate drugs. And let's also, for the sake of argument, put aside the fact that US subversion and aggression continue to lead to increase of production and use of drugs. On these charitable assumptions, US operations in Colombia are truly scandalous. That seems transparent. To bring the point out more clearly, consider the fact, not in dispute, that deaths from tobacco vastly exceed those from all hard drugs combined. Furthermore, hard drugs harm the user, while tobacco harms others – not as much, to be sure, as alcohol, which is heavily implicated in killing of others (automobile accidents, alcohol-induced violence, etc.), but significantly. Deaths from 'passive smoking' probably exceed those from all hard drugs combined, and 'soft drugs' that are severely criminalized, like marijuana, while doubtless harmful (like coffee, red meat, etc.), are not known to have significant lethal effects. Furthermore, while the Colombian cartels are not permitted to place billboards in Times Square, New York, or run ads on TV, to induce children and other vulnerable sectors of the population to use cocaine and heroin, there are no such barriers against advertising for the far more lethal tobacco-based products, and in fact countries have been threatened with serious trade sanctions if they violate the sacred principles of 'free trade' by attempting to regulate such practices. An elementary conclusion follows at once: if the USA is entitled to carry out chemical warfare targeting poor peasants in Colombia, then Colombia, and China, and many others, are surely entitled to carry out far more extensive chemical warfare programmes targeting agribusiness production in North Carolina and Kentucky. Comment should be unnecessary.

Colombia has a violent history, in large part rooted in the fact that its great natural wealth and opportunities are monopolized by narrow, privileged and often quite brutal sectors, while much of the population lives in misery and endures severe repression. Colombia's tragic history took a new turn, however, in the early 1960s, when US intervention became a much more significant factor – not that it had been marginal before, for example, when Theodore Roosevelt stole part of Colombia for a canal that was of great importance for US economic and strategic interests. In 1962, John F. Kennedy in effect shifted the mission of the Latin American military from 'hemispheric defense', a residue of the

Second World War , to 'internal security', a euphemism for war against the domestic population.

There were significant effects throughout Latin America. One consequence in Colombia, as Stokes reviews, was the official US recommendation to rely on paramilitary terror against 'known communist proponents'. The effects on Colombia were described by the president of the Colombian Permanent Committee for Human Rights, the distinguished diplomat Alfredo Vàzquez Carrizosa. Beyond the crimes that are institutionalized in the 'dual structure of a prosperous minority and an impoverished, excluded majority, with great differences in wealth, income, and access to political participation', he wrote, the Kennedy initiatives led to an 'exacerbation of violence by external factors', as Washington 'took great pains to transform our regular armies into counterinsurgency brigades, accepting the new strategy of the death squads', decisions that 'ushered in what is known in Latin America as the National Security Doctrine'. This was not 'defense against an external enemy, but a way to make the military establishment the masters of the game ... [with] the right to combat the internal enemy, as set forth in the Brazilian doctrine, the Argentine doctrine, the Uruguayan doctrine, and the Colombian doctrine: it is the right to fight and to exterminate social workers, trade unionists, men and women who are not supportive of the establishment, and who are assumed to be communist extremists' – a term with wide coverage in CI lingo, including human rights activists, priests organizing peasants, labour leaders, others seeking to address the 'dual structure' by non-violent democratic means, and of course the great mass of victims of the dual structure, if they dare to raise their heads.

The policy was certainly not new. The horrifying example of Guatemala is sufficient to show that. Nor was it restricted to Latin America. In many ways, the early post-war CI operations in Greece (with some 150,000 dead) and South Korea (with a death toll of 100,000) had set the pattern long before. Apart from its Guatemala atrocities, the Eisenhower administration had overthrown the parliamentary government of Iran and restored the brutal rule of the Shah in order to bar Iran from taking control of its own resources, and, in 1958, had carried out some of the most extreme post-war clandestine operations in its effort to undermine the parliamentary government of Indonesia, which was becoming dangerously democratic, and to split off the outer islands, where most of the resources were – just to mention a few examples. But there was a qualitative change in the early 1960s.

In Latin America, the Kennedy administration orchestrated a military coup in Brazil, which took place shortly after Kennedy's assassination, installing the first of the National Security States, complete with large-scale torture, destruction of popular organizations and any vestige of democracy, and intense repression. It was welcomed in Washington as a 'democratic rebellion', 'a great victory for free world', which prevented a 'total loss to the West of all South American Republics' and should 'create a greatly improved climate for private investments'. The democratic revolution carried out by the neo-Nazi generals was 'the single most decisive victory of freedom in the mid-twentieth century', Kennedy's Ambassador Lincoln Gordon held, 'one of the major turning points in world history' in this period. Shortly after, the Indonesian problem was dealt with successfully as General Suharto took over in a military coup, with a 'staggering mass slaughter', as the *New York Times* described the outcome, 'a gleam of light in Asia', in the words of their leading liberal commentator, James Reston. As was known at once, the death toll was immense, perhaps half a million or many more, mostly landless peasants. The threat of excessive democracy that had troubled the Eisenhower administration was overcome, with the destruction of the major mass-based political party in the country, which 'had won widespread support not as a revolutionary party [despite its name: PKI, Indonesian Communist Party] but as an organization defending the interests of the poor within the existing system', Australian Indonesia specialist Harold Crouch observes, developing a 'mass base among the peasantry' through its 'vigor in defending the interests of the … poor'. Western euphoria was irrepressible, and continued as Suharto compiled one of the worst human rights records of the late twentieth century, also invading East Timor and carrying out a near-genocidal slaughter, with firm support from the USA and UK, among others, to the bloody end in late 1999. The gleam of light in Indonesia also eliminated one of the pillars of the hated non-aligned movement. A second was eliminated when Israel destroyed Nasser's army in 1967, firmly establishing the US–Israeli alliance that has persisted since.

In Latin America, the Brazilian coup had a domino effect, as the National Security Doctrine spread throughout the continent with varying degrees of US initiative, but constant and decisive support, however terrible the consequences. One example is 'the first 9/11', in Chile, 11 September 1973, when General Pinochet's forces bombed the presidential palace and demolished Latin America's oldest and most vibrant democracy, establishing a regime of torture and repression thanks primarily to the secret police organization DINA that US military intelligence compared to the KGB and the Gestapo – while Washington firmly supported the regime. The official death toll of the first 9/11 was 3,200, which would correspond to about 50,000 in the USA; the actual toll was doubtless much higher. Pinochet's DINA soon moved to integrate Latin American dictatorships in the international state terrorist programme 'Operation Condor', which killed and tortured mercilessly within the countries and branched out to terrorist operations in Europe and the USA. The evil genius, Pinochet, was greatly honoured, by Reagan and Thatcher in particular, but quite generally. The assassination of a respected diplomat in Washington was going too far, however, and Operation Condor was wound down. The worst atrocities, in Argentina, were yet to come, along with the expansion of the state terror to Central America in the 1980s, leaving hundreds of thousands of corpses and four countries in ruins, along with a condemnation of the USA by the World Court for its 'unlawful use of force' (in lay terms, international terrorism), backed by two (vetoed) Security Council resolutions, after which Washington escalated the terror to new heights. Colombia's travail was part of a far broader picture.

US terror operations in Central America were accompanied by expansion of the drug trade, the usual concomitant of international terrorism, which relies crucially on criminal elements and untraceable financial resources – meaning narcotics. Washington's mobilization of radical Islamists in Afghanistan, in collaboration with Pakistani intelligence and other allies, led to a far larger explosion of drug production and narco-trafficking, with lethal effects in the region and far beyond. These US policies proceeded side by side with the 'drug war' at home and in Colombia, no embarrassing questions raised. Drug production and distribution are rapidly increasing in Afghanistan and Kosovo, consistent with the traditional pattern, while Colombian peasants suffer and die from chemical warfare attacks and are driven to urban slums where they can rot alongside millions of others in one of the world's largest refugee catastrophes. And in the USA, drugs remain available with no change, the measures that are known to be effective in dealing with drug problems (let alone the social conditions in which they arise) are scarcely pursued, and victims flow from urban slums to the flourishing prison-industrial complex, as some criminologists call it.

The mass murderers and torturers of the Latin American National Security States have sometimes had to face at least public inquiries into their crimes. Some have even faced the bar of justice, though nothing remotely like what would be appropriate to such crimes by Western standards. Others, however, are completely immune. In the major study of Operation Condor, journalist/analyst John Dinges observes: 'Only in the United States, whose diplomats, intelligence, and military were so intimately intertwined with the military dictators and their operational subordinates, has there been judicial silence on the crimes of the Condor years.' The United States, he continues, 'conferred on itself a kind of de facto amnesty even more encompassing than that enjoyed by its Latin American allies: no truth commissions or any other kind of official investigation was established to look into the human collateral damage of the many proxy wars that were supported in Latin America or elsewhere' – and, we may add, actual wars, including horrendous crimes, shielded by the same self-declared amnesty.

The powerful are, typically, immune to prosecution or even serious inquiry, even memory for that matter. Only their citizens can end such crimes, and the far more terrible crimes that flow from permanent immunity.

As Stokes reviews in convincing detail, US policies persist while pretexts and tactics shift as circumstances require. Sometimes the basic principles are frankly stated. Thus diplomatic historian Gerald Haines (also senior historian of the CIA) introduces his study of 'the Americanization of Brazil' by observing that 'Following World War II the United States assumed, out of self-interest, responsibility for the welfare of the world capitalist system' – which does not mean the welfare of the people of the system, as events were to prove, not surprisingly. The enemy was 'communism'. The reasons were outlined by a prestigious study group of the Woodrow Wilson Foundation and the National Planning Association in a comprehensive 1955 study on the political economy of US foreign policy: the primary threat of communism, the study concluded, is the economic transformation of the communist powers 'in ways that reduce their willingness and ability to complement the industrial economies of the West'. It makes good sense, then, that prospects of independent development should be regarded as a serious danger, to be pre-empted by violence if necessary. That is particularly true if the errant society shows signs of success in terms that might be meaningful to others suffering from similar oppression and injustice. In that case it becomes a 'virus' that might 'infect others', a 'rotten apple' that might 'spoil the barrel', in the terminology of top planners, describing the real domino theory, not the version fabricated to frighten the domestic public into obedience.

The Cold War itself had similar characteristics, taking on a life of its own because of scale. That is implicitly recognized by leading establishment scholars, notably John Lewis Gaddis, regarded as the dean of Cold War scholarship. He plausibly traces the origins of the Cold War to 1917, when Russia broke free of its relations of semi-colonial depend-ency on the West and sought to pursue an independent course. Gaddis articulates fundamental principles perceptively when he regards the very existence of the Bolshevik regime as a form of aggression, so that the intervention of the Western powers was actually self-defence, undertaken 'in response to a profound and potentially far-reaching intervention by the new Soviet government in the internal affairs, not just of the West, but of virtually every country in the world', namely, 'the Revolution's challenge – which could hardly have been more categorical – to the very survival of the capitalist order'. Change of the social order in Russia and announcement of intentions to spread the model elsewhere are aggression that elicits invasion as justified self-defence.

The threat that Russia could prove to be a 'virus' was very real, Woodrow Wilson and Lloyd George recognized, not only in the colonial world but even in the rich industrial societies. Those concerns remained very much alive into the 1960s, we know from the internal record. It should come as no surprise, then, that these thoughts are reiterated over and over, as when Kennedy–Johnson high-level planners warned that the 'very existence' of the Castro regime in Cuba was 'successful defiance' of US policies going back to the Monroe Doctrine, so that the 'terrors of the earth' must be visited on Cuba, to borrow the phrase of historian and Kennedy confidant Arthur Schlesinger, describing the prime goal of Robert Kennedy, who was assigned responsibility for the terrorist operations.

Colombia, again, falls well within a much more general pattern, though in each case, the horrors that are endured are terrible in their own special and indescribable ways.

To Eric, a good friend and scholar

I | Introduction: interpreting US foreign policy in Colombia

During the Cold War the US intervened in more states in Latin America than in any other continent, with US-sponsored counter-insurgency (CI) the primary means of US coercive statecraft.[1] US planners argued that CI support for allied states was designed to contain the influence of the Soviet Union through the destruction of left-wing armed insurgencies that were portrayed as externally sponsored instances of Soviet expansionism. Throughout this period Colombia remained one of the largest recipients of US CI funding and training designed to destroy the Revolutionary Armed Forces of Colombia (FARC), a rebel insurgency movement. The FARC were portrayed as Soviet-backed guerrillas, and as a threat to the pro-US Colombian state. During these years of support, the Colombian military carried out widespread human rights abuses. Although these abuses were not publicly approved, they were considered a necessary evil required to prevent the alleged devastating consequences to US security should a potentially pro-Soviet state come to power in Latin America.[2] George Kennan, the architect of the USA's Cold War grand strategy of containment, explained that in dealing with communism in Latin America the final answer 'may be an unpleasant one' but the USA 'should not hesitate before police repression by the local government'. Kennan considered this repression not only to be strategically necessary but also to be ethically correct, as 'the Communists are essentially traitors'. He continued, it 'is better to have a strong regime in power than a liberal government if it is indulgent and relaxed and penetrated by Communists'.[3]

Interestingly, with the end of the Cold War the USA has not only continued to fund and train the Colombian military for its fight against the FARC, but has dramatically escalated its support to the extent that Colombia is now the third largest recipient of US military aid in the world.[4] A central question emerges from this account, and it is the puzzle that this book attempts to answer: given the high human costs historically associated with US Cold War support for abusive Latin American militaries, *why has US aid to the Colombian military been continued throughout the post-Cold War period?* This question is especially pertinent given the justifications employed by the USA during the Cold War era, the USA's publicly declared commitment to post-Cold War democracy promotion and humanitarian intervention to prevent human rights abuses,[5] and the continuing record of gross human rights abuses committed by the Colombian military and their paramilitary allies who are responsible for over 70 per cent of all politically motivated assassinations.[6]

In seeking to explore these issues, this book relates this continuity in US military funding to a wider set of debates within the discipline of International Relations (IR). Specifically, within IR, a *discontinuity* thesis has emerged that views US post-Cold War objectives within the Third World as significantly different from their earlier Cold War orientation. This book formulates an alternative *continuity* thesis and argues, in contrast, that in the case of Colombia US objectives and policy are characterized by significant continuity with their earlier Cold War orientation. This interpretive dichotomy between the discontinuity and continuity arguments animates the empirical analysis of US policy in Colombia. In relation to US intervention in Colombia, the discontinuity thesis is deeply rooted within mainstream academia, the international media and the US policy community. The switch from the objectives of Cold War containment of communist insurgency using CI to an allegedly new counter-narcotic and counter-terrorist orientation are taken as both the principal indicators of discontinuity in US policy and objectives, and as the primary justification for the continued funding of the Colombian military, albeit for the new post-Cold War battles against drugs and terrorism.

In opposition to the discontinuity thesis, this book constructs a continuity argument and grounds this empirically by showing that the USA is neither targeting the primary drug traffickers nor fighting a war on international terrorism in Colombia. Instead, the USA has continued to fund and train the Colombian military for a CI war against both the Colombian insurgents and progressive sections of Colombian civil society throughout the post-Cold War era. As such, the wars on drugs and terrorism provide a pretext for this continuity of US CI strategy, and US post-Cold War objectives form an overarching continuity with their earlier Cold War policy and objectives. This continuity is due to the fact that US economic and strategic interests in Colombia have remained the same, and the Colombian case grounds a wider critical perspective as to the nature of US foreign and security policy within the new world order.

This book thus refutes the rhetorical claims of US policy-makers and the mainstream discontinuity arguments as to the nature of US intervention in Colombia, while exploring the role that the USA has played in installing, codifying and supporting Colombian state terrorism both during and after the Cold War period. The central argument is that the USA *continues to pursue a pervasive strategy of state terrorism in Colombia to protect its economic and political interests in South America*. This goes against the vast majority of analyses of US policy in Colombia, which maintain that the USA has been fighting a war on drugs, and now a new 'war on terror' in Colombia, and not war *of* terror designed to destroy both armed and unarmed social forces. There are three main reasons for this continuity.

First, the USA's war on drugs and the new war on terror are pretexts used to justify the continued funding of the Colombian military so that it can pacify those armed groups and unarmed progressive social forces that potentially threaten a stability geared towards US interests. These interests have remained consistent with the Cold War period. Furthermore, not only is the USA not fighting a war on drugs and on terrorism, but it is actually sponsoring the principal drug-funded terrorists in Colombia through its use of CI warfare.

Second, in the wake of the Gulf War in 1990 and the events of September 11 2001, the USA has sought to diversify its oil purchasing from the Middle East to other sources. Colombia's neighbour, Venezuela, is currently one of the largest oil suppliers to US markets, with Colombia supplying more oil to the USA today than Kuwait did prior to the first Gulf War. US planners have explicitly linked South American regional security to the instability in Colombia and have asserted the importance of US strategic oil acquisition needs in driving US intervention in Colombia. US access to South American oil thus contributes to the continued funding of the Colombian military for CI.

Third, a prevailing CI discourse exists that continues to construct the identity of various elements of civil society such as unions, teachers' organizations, human rights groups and so on as 'subversive'. This book unpacks this discourse using US military manuals and doctrine and relates it to the evolution of US CI warfare during the Cold War and the way it continues to be mapped on to the Colombian situation. The continued existence of these US economic and strategic interests provides the most plausible account of the continuity of post-Cold War US intervention in Colombia alongside the continued existence of the CI discourse which affects the way the war is waged in Colombia.

Colombia occupies the north-western part of South America and shares borders with Panama, Venezuela, Brazil, Peru and Ecuador. It also possesses coasts on both the Pacific Ocean and Caribbean Sea while its three Andean mountain ranges split the country into climatically distinct areas with the Amazon rainforest to the south, vast barren plains to the east and the Caribbean coast to the north. Alongside its geographical diversity Colombia is racially mixed and traces its various ethnicities from its own indigenous peoples, the early Spanish colonizers and the African slaves put to work on its colonial plantations. By the early nineteenth century 50 per cent of Colombia's people were of mixed race. Politically, Colombia prides itself on being one of Latin America's oldest democracies, with the Republic of Colombia established in 1886. Since its inception, however, Colombia has been characterized by extreme class stratification, social exclusion and political violence. Politically these tensions have been refracted through the rivalries of Colombia's two main parties: the Conservatives and Liberals. Both parties have dominated Colombia's political system since their formation in the 1840s with the Conservatives pro-Church, anti-reform and closely aligned with the landholding class while the Liberals have tended to pursue modest social reforms and have aligned with Colombia's commercial sectors. Aside from these differences, however, the desire to resist fundamental change to Colombia's prevailing socio-economic system has tended to unite them with both parties relying upon clientelistic networks to entrench their power at local level. Importantly, both have been united in their opposition to social forces that have sought to reform Colombia's highly unequal economy which has long been characterized by extreme divisions of wealth. Today, for example, Colombia has one of the most unequal divisions in the world. The UN states that 10 per cent of Colombia's rich have a 46.1 per cent share of national income. Conversely, the poorest 10 per cent have 1.1 per cent.[7] Colombia is thus effectively characterized by two economies: one formal and one informal, and it is the vast and precarious informal economy that sustains the livelihoods of the majority of Colombia's urban population.

One of the central bulwarks against economic reformism has been the Colombian military which has long acted to insulate the Colombian political and economic system from popular pressures for reform.[8] This relationship was codified under the National Front arrangement of the 1950s which alternated power between Conservative and Liberal elites, and which effectively continues to this day. It was under the National Front that the Colombian military was given *carte blanche* to eradicate enclaves of peasant colonizers in Colombia's south left over from a brutal civil war now called simply *la violencia* ('the violence') that claimed up to 300,000 lives. The colonizers were fleeing the persecution of Colombia's landholding oligarchy and it was these same colonizers that would later go on to form the FARC, the longest running rebel insurgency movement in Latin America's history. It was also under the National Front arrangement that the USA stepped up its commitments to Colombia as part of its new Cold War crusade of anti-communism. This period of US intervention marked a watershed in Colombian and US relations, with the Colombian military consistently remaining one of the largest recipients of US military aid and training throughout the Cold War. It was also the first country in Latin America to adopt US CI measures in relation to its perceived problems of insurgency and civil unrest and also hosted the first Latin America counter-insurgency training school.[9]

By the late 1960s Colombia's military was firmly under the guidance of the USA. A 1969 Colombian CI manual lists eight US CI manuals as sources, combined with anthologies of articles published in the US *Military Review*.[10] Colombia has also sent more students to the US CI training academy, the School of the Americas (SOA), than any other Latin American nation.[11] Importantly, the Colombian military still maintains extensive ties to the USA, and is by far the largest recipient of US military aid in Latin America, and the third largest in the world. Despite these continuing ties, US objectives in Colombia are popularly viewed to have switched dramatically from anti-communist CI to a counter-narcotic war on drugs and, more recently, on terror. However, as Nazih Richani argues, there is a relative dearth of studies on Colombia, and this extends to substantive studies on US policy towards Colombia, particularly from more critical perspectives.[12] Given the ongoing and massive levels of commitment on the part of the USA, coupled with the levels of violence and human rights abuses committed in the Colombian conflict, this book is an attempt to plug this gap and is thus primarily an examination of US policy in Colombia.

In relation to existing literatures on US foreign policy in Colombia, some taxonomic ordering is inevitable. Although this sometimes does violence to the subtle differences between thinkers and theories, it also provides a useful mechanism for revealing patterns. Broadly speaking, the different perspectives on US policy in Colombia both during and after the Cold War fall into two camps. The first is the mainstream camp, which is largely supportive of US policies and objectives in Colombia. This perspective is by far the largest, and spans the English-language academic literature, the American media and the US policy-making community. The second set of literature is critical of US policy and is much smaller. This set includes some academic literature, but rarely finds its way into the American media or the US policy-making community. This book falls clearly into the critical camp.

As Robert Pastor notes, within the majority of mainstream academic approaches to the study of US foreign policy towards Latin America there are two main strands, conservative and liberal:

> Conservatives focus on a relatively narrower idea of US interests and a military based definition of power. They believe that the United States should approach problems unilaterally and in a practical and forceful-solving manner. Liberals give higher priority to the moral dimension and to ... 'soft power,' which derives from the American model. They look at social and economic causes of the crisis, try to understand the issues from the other's perspective, and rely on multilateral, diplomatic approaches.[13]

This distinction between mainstream liberal and conservative approaches provides a useful way of thinking through the differences between analysts on Colombia. Conservatives tend to emphasize military solutions to Colombia's conflict, view the Colombian military as the best way of implementing US interests, and see no ethical issues arising as a result of continued US support for the Colombian military. For example, Richard Downes argues that drug trafficking in Colombia jeopardizes the national security interests of the USA, with the 'impact of the drug industry ... devastating on US society'. He subsequently calls for an active military engagement with Colombia's 'narco-guerrillas' through the intensification of US military aid.[14] David Passage also advocates an increase of US military aid to Colombia so as to help 'Colombia's democratically elected government regain control of its national territory' which can then 'halt the production of illegal narcotics' which threaten US national security interests.[15] Angel Rabasa and Peter Chalk argue that US national security considerations are as significant as its alleged counter-narcotics concerns in Colombia, and trace this to Colombia's geostrategic importance. Both Rabasa and Chalk call for the USA to upgrade and modernize the Colombian military to regain control of Colombia's rural areas and to contain regional destabilization.[16] Dennis Rempe's work begins by arguing that throughout the Cold War the US 'pursued an indirect policy that played to America's strengths: economic and military aid, training of security forces, technical assistance, and logistical and intelligence support' which furthered 'US Cold War interests'.[17] Rempe continues that the primary threats to US interests in post-Cold War Colombia now come from illegal narcotics, with US policy switching from a strategy of anti-communist CI to a new war on drugs. Rempe states that US policy combines both 'counter-narcotics and institution-building strategies with a negotiated settlement to that nation's long-running insurgent war'.[18] In fighting the war on drugs, Rempe cautions that Colombian policy-makers must 'concentrate security efforts on neutralizing the clandestine infrastructure and military power' of Colombia's 'narco-guerrillas'. He also recommends the incorporation of Colombia's clandestine paramilitary networks within an overall security system so as to improve the capacity for the war on drugs to eliminate the alleged interweaved problems of insurgency and narcotics trafficking.[19]

In the aftermath of September 11, US policy has increasingly been justified as both a war on drugs and a new war on terrorism, and the USA has continued to provide large-scale funding and training for the Colombian military. For example, Colombia was by far the largest recipient of US military training in 2002, with 3.6 times more soldiers trained than Thailand, the second largest.[20] In justifying the continued funding of the Colombian military, the US Assistant Secretary of State for Western Hemisphere Affairs, Otto Reich, argued that the '40 million people of Colombia deserve freedom from terror and an opportunity to participate fully in the new democratic community of American states. It is in our self-interest to see that they get it.'[21] As such, the emphasis has continued to be placed upon a militarized solution to Colombia's internal violence. Although it is as yet too early for substantive academic studies on the way in which the USA's war on terror has affected its Colombian policy, the continuity of emphasis on militarized solutions has been reflected in the media. For example, the *Washington Post* argues that US military aid should now be delinked from its supposed exclusive focus on counter-narcotics and the USA should ease its human rights requirement on the Colombian military so as better to prosecute the new war on terror: 'US military assistance and equipment, including 50 helicopters, can be used only against drug traffickers, not guerrillas. The congressional Democrats who have insisted on the restrictions have justified this policy by citing the army's human rights record.' It continues that US policy-makers should ease the human rights conditions so that 'the United States' can 'come to [the] defense' of this 'moderate democracy in the heart of the Americas'.[22] Conservatives thus view US military aid to Colombia as the best way of securing US interests, and either ignore or downplay the human rights consequences of US policy. The primary threat to US interests during the Cold War was seen as communist insurgents; drugs and terrorism are the new post-Cold War threats.

The liberal approach, while not challenging the characterization of Cold War US policy as driven by bipolar competition or post-Cold War

US policy as driven by drugs and counter-terrorism, tends to advocate a more multi-layered and less overtly militarized approach for US policy than the more conservative approaches outlined above. It is also more critical of US policy. However, it tends to couch this criticism in terms of US policy shortcomings and argues that while US intervention in Colombia is a good thing, the USA should stress human rights and economic development *as well as* the war on drugs and terror. Indicative of this approach is Raphael Perl, who castigates the US militarization of the war on drugs in Colombia. Perl argues that the USA 'is *inadvertently* strengthening the power of the military at the expense of often fragile, civilian democratic institutions in the region', which threatens to harm human rights in Colombia.[23] Similarly, Roberto Steiner accepts that during the Cold War 'US involvement in Latin America was more closely linked to containing the spread of communism than to combating drugs'.[24] He goes on to condemn the overt militarized focus of US policy in Colombia and argues that the US–Colombian 'bilateral anti-drug agenda has proven to be remarkably unsuccessful' because drugs have become more available in the USA, while 'Colombia's income from drugs has stabilized'.[25] Furthermore, Steiner argues that the overtly militarized focus of US policy could have the potential to lead to human rights abuses in Colombia. However, Steiner tempers his concern and argues that: '[t]he good news is, of course ... human rights abuses now rank very high in the US agenda.'[26] Thus, human rights abuses committed by the US-backed Colombian military are seen as an aberration from an otherwise correct US policy of military funding, with US policy moving to address these problems through its alleged strict human rights conditions and the professionalization of the Colombian military.

A common theme among liberal approaches to US policy is how the USA's alleged war on drugs after the Cold War in Colombia has failed to stem the level of drugs entering the USA itself. Critics thus argue that the USA should continue to fund the Colombian military but should simultaneously pursue economic and social solutions or concentrate on both supply side (Colombian) and demand side (US) reduction efforts. The failure of the USA's 'war on drugs' in Colombia is traced to a number of different factors. For example, in his book *Cocaine Quagmire*, Sewall Menzel argues that while the funding of the Colombian military was correct, the US war on drugs in Colombia has failed largely because it has ignored the social and economic issues.[27] Similarly, Ron Chepesiuk argues that US objectives in its war on drugs are unclear with bureaucratic infighting hampering the effective implementation of the USA's counter-narcotic strategy,[28] while Patrick Clawson and Rensselaer Lee argue that US intervention in Colombia has failed to stem the amount of drugs entering the USA.[29] Drexler also condemns the failure of US narcotics eradication in Colombia while cautioning against the human rights abuses within Colombia itself: 'Washington needs to state that it understands that abuses of human rights are contrary to longstanding policies of the Colombian government, but that it shares the conviction of a wide, influential number of Americans that stronger measures must be taken against such violations.'[30] Bruce Bagley and Juan Tokatlian go so far as to argue that the reason the US war on drugs has failed is largely because it is premised on realist assumptions on the part of US policy-makers. They argue that by taking the state as the central unit of analysis in world politics, US policy-makers have failed to grasp the fact that 'multiple subnational and transnational actors are involved in the international [drug] industry [that] operate outside, if not in direct defiance, of national authorities throughout the hemisphere'.[31] They also argue that the notion that the US military is the best way of waging the so-called war on drugs reflects 'the realists' consistent overestimation of the efficacy of force as an instrument of policy'.[32]

Most illustrative of the liberal approach is the work of Russell Crandall, who has produced the most extensive body of work on US post-Cold War policy in Colombia. His *Driven by Drugs* argues that US post-Cold War policy in Colombia was, indeed, driven by drugs. According to Crandall, US concerns throughout the Cold War were dominated by the 'threat of Communist infiltration and expansion in the region'.[33] In the post-Cold War era, however, Crandall argues that 'intermestic' concerns – that is, a combination of both domestic and international priorities – have come to dominate US policy towards Colombia. Crandall argues that domestically the USA was becoming increasingly concerned with drug use, while internationally it sought to pursue a strategy of drug eradication in the source countries. As with the analysts outlined above, Crandall argues that the USA supply-side war on drugs in Colombia has failed to stem the flow of drugs into the USA. In response, Crandall argues that the USA has chosen radically to escalate its counter-drug assistance to Colombia in the form of 'Plan Colombia', a $1.3 billion military aid package which mostly goes to Colombia. Crandall states: 'Washington's solution for "saving" Colombia, that is, the component of Plan Colombia provided by the United States, was essentially a series of counter-narcotics measures. Plan Colombia was thus the ideal justification for what was basically an extension of the war on drugs.'[34]

Crandall's overall thesis is that prior to September 11 drugs were the 'overriding priority' of the USA in Colombia.[35] He argues that with the election of George W. Bush, and after September 11, there has been a change in US policy towards a more counter-terrorist orientation: 'The new anti-terror climate in Washington will certainly influence how the Bush administration views the new dynamics in Colombia ... it is increasingly likely that the US government ... will view FARC kidnappings, murders, and bombings more as "terrorist" activities than acts of war.'[36] In pursuing the new agenda, Crandall cautions that Washington should wait for the Colombians themselves to come up with ways of ending the violence in Colombia. This will avoid the perception that the USA wishes to 'solve Colombia's problems more than Colombia does'.[37]

In summary, the primary differences between conservative and liberal mainstream analysts of US policy in Colombia are their policy prescriptions and relative critical orientations. Conservatives tend to favour militarized solutions to perceived problems. US military aid to the Colombian military is thus seen as the best way of achieving US national interests. Liberals, on the other hand, tend to emphasize a mixture of social, economic and military responses to Colombia's problems, and view the Colombian military as in need of some reform. In relation to human rights abuses in Colombia (if they are mentioned at all), conservatives tend to see them as a result of the violence committed by armed insurgents and advocate a militarized approach to eradicate the 'narco-guerrillas' who protect Colombia's coca plantations. On the other hand, liberals tend to concede that the Colombian military also commits human rights abuses, and in response either calls for more social and economic aid, or more effective US military aid and training to professionalize the Colombian military. Rarely, is *any* mention made of the relationship between US policy and the levels of violence in Colombia. If it is mentioned it is seen as an aberration, a policy failure or a mistake and not as a systematic pattern. Thus, mainstream analysts couch their criticism within a narrative of US policy failure or the unintentional consequences of an otherwise correct policy of US funding for the Colombian military. Beyond these differences are a far larger set of shared assumptions such as the belief that US policy was driven by a bipolar security logic during the Cold War, and that the threats to US national security interests have switched to counter-narcotics and counter-terrorism during the post-Cold War era. This switch allegedly indicates a discontinuity in US objectives within Colombia. Furthermore, both conservatives and liberals do not challenge the belief that the USA has an innate right to continue to intervene in Colombia and the essentially benign nature of US policy. As Crandall argues, while 'some US policymakers expressed concern over the human rights implications and the lack of an exit strategy, the main disagreements' between liberals and conservatives arose 'not over *whether* to send helicopters' to Colombia, but 'over *how many* should be sent'.[38]

In contrast to these mainstream approaches, more critical approaches to US policy in Colombia tend to argue that US post-Cold War policy and objectives in Colombia continue to be characterized by a prevailing CI strategy aimed at destroying threats to US economic and political interests. Critical approaches thus reject the mainstream view that the overriding priority of the USA in the post-Cold War era is either a war on drugs or a new war on terrorism, and draw a link between the continued use of CI warfare, and the preservation of a capitalist socio-economic order conducive to US interests. George Monbiot summarizes the position very clearly. On the effect of US intervention in Colombia, Monbiot argues that officially the US 'is now involved there in a "war on terror". Before September 2001, it was a "war on drugs"; before that, a "war on communism". In essence, however, US intervention in Colombia is unchanged: this remains, as it has always been, a war on the poor.'[39]

Furthermore, critically inclined analysts draw a direct link between US policy in Colombia and human rights abuses, and do not frame these abuses as either aberrations or mistakes, but as a systematic pattern of repression designed to protect capitalism in Colombia. For example, Peter Wilkin examines US policy in Colombia and argues that the 'core capitalist liberal states are using the means of violence as a mechanism for promoting social change in a way that far exceeds the worst excesses of any non-state terrorist actors'. In contrast to the mainstream approaches, he also questions the alleged US war on drugs and states that the primary '"narco-terrorists" are the drug gangs and the paramilitaries, who exist in a mutually supportive relationship with the Colombian state'.[40] Similarly, James Petras argues that US funding for the Colombian military is designed primarily to destroy the left-wing FARC guerrillas on the pretext of waging a war on drugs. As such, the US military aid package, Plan Colombia, was in fact an 'attempt to behead the most advanced radicalized and well-organized opposition to US hemispheric hegemony'.[41] Javier Giraldo documents the strategy used for the destruction of the FARC, which involves the pervasive use of paramilitaries to wage a 'dirty-war' on the FARC and their alleged civilian sympathizers. His work thus draws a link between the use of CI by the USA and human rights abuses through illustrating the centrality of paramilitarism to the USA's overall strategy.[42] In a nuanced account of Colombia's violence, Nazih Richani argues that the war between the Colombian state and the guerrilla movements has sedimented their relations into a 'war system'. US intervention, especially the escalation of military funding contained within Plan Colombia, threatens to 'exacerbate the civil war augmenting the cost of its continuation'.[43] Robin Kirk's more autobiographical approach also explicitly draws the link between US policy and human rights abuses in Colombia. Kirk notes that when US policy-makers were told that US military funding would be used for CI by senior Colombian military personnel, the 'announcement caused little comment, a sign of how neatly the war on subversion had already melded into the "war on drugs" … Colombia's use of US funds and advice, and the human rights abuses that resulted, caused little outrage in Washington.'[44] Similarly, Noam Chomsky provides an analysis of the continued use of US CI strategy to pacify both Colombian civil society and its armed groups.[45] Chomsky begins by highlighting the extensive collusion between the Colombian military and paramilitary networks throughout Colombia. These paramilitaries commit the vast majority of human rights abuses.[46] By extension, then, Chomsky argues that by funding the Colombian military, the USA is also supporting Colombia's paramilitary groups and is thus deeply implicated in human rights abuses. Moreover, the USA funds the Colombian military so as to defend its economic interests: 'The targets of the Colombia Plan are guerrilla forces based on the peasantry and calling for internal social change, which would interfere with integration of Colombia into the global system on the terms that the USA demands: dominated by elites linked to US power interests …'[47] Chomsky explicitly associates US military aid to Colombia with the preservation of particular socio-economic relations that benefit US economic and strategic elite interests and sections of the Colombian ruling class. US-backed CI aid and training to Colombia thus form part of a 'long history of driving peasants off the land for the benefit of wealthy elites and resource extraction by foreign investors'.[48]

While all of the critical scholars above make reference to US Cold War policy in Colombia, none of them has examined it in any great detail.[49] In particular none of the critical scholarship has made any significant reference to the initial stages of US CI intervention in Colombia in the early 1960s. During this crucial period the USA reoriented the Colombian military to an overtly internal security role reliant on a CI strategy. Chapter 2 explores the nature of this earlier period in US policy towards Colombia, and makes use of a number of recently declassified documents relating to US policy during this crucial period.[50] Also, there are a number of gaps in the historiographical literature in relation to the immediate post-Cold War period prior to Plan Colombia. This book incorporates a number of declassified documents released in 2002 which relate directly to US policy in Colombia.[51] These documents in turn provide an insight into the thinking of US planners and how US policy unfolded prior to the major escalation of US military funding under Plan Colombia.[52]

The next chapter provides the broad framework of analysis for understanding US intervention in Latin America generally and Colombia more specifically. It outlines the evolution of the US Cold War containment strategy in Latin America and the justifications given for US intervention, and shows how an orthodox historiography of US foreign relations underpins mainstream IR's presumptions as to the nature of US intervention with US foreign policy in Latin America overwhelmingly interpreted as defensively driven by security considerations related to the bipolar competition. In contrast stand revisionist historical perspectives that relate US Cold War foreign and security policy to the maintenance of a world capitalist order conducive to US economic interests. The Latin American case studies examined in this chapter show clearly that US planners *principally* feared the threat of Latin American states pursuing majoritarian development policies and not Soviet expansionism and thus confirm revisionist perspectives.

Chapter 3 examines discontinuity arguments in relation to the nature of post-Cold War US foreign and security policy and contrasts US post-Cold War policy justifications with policy practice and its effects. It is clear that US objectives have indeed remained the same as their earlier Cold War orientation.

Chapter 4 focuses on US policy in Colombia during the Cold War and examines the way in which US intervention orientated the Colombian state towards an internal security role through the formalization of state terrorism as a necessary response to indigenous insurgency. This formalization took place at both the level of training, and also at the ideological level, with the inculcation of a 'CI discourse' within recipient militaries that specifically portrayed progressive sections of civil society as inimical to the overall CI effort. In outlining the CI discourse, a number of US military manuals are examined. These manuals were used by the USA throughout the Cold War period to train militaries for CI. This chapter then examines the ways in which the USA's CI strategy and discourse were implemented in Colombia during the Cold War.

Chapter 5 details the switch in US justifications for its continued support of the Colombian military after the Cold War, from a justification of anti-communist containment to a new 'war on drugs' and, after September 11, to the 'war on terrorism'. Primary and secondary data sources show that despite such claims the USA has in fact continued to pursue a pervasive strategy of CI aimed primarily at the FARC and Colombian civil society. Concomitantly, this strategy continues to lead to widespread human rights abuses and constitutes a major continuity with the earlier Cold War period. Furthermore, the US is in fact relying upon the biggest drug traffickers and terrorists in Colombia to implement this strategy. This chapter thus empirically grounds the overall continuity argument in relation to US post-Cold War policy in Colombia.

Chapter 6 then draws together the case study findings in order to reach substantive conclusions regarding the causal link between US interests and the continuity of US-sponsored CI in Colombia. There are three primary reasons for the continuity of US post-Cold War policy in Colombia: the preservation of a capitalist international order, US access to strategic natural resources, and the continuity of the CI discourse which continues to construct social relations between the Colombian state and civil society in particular ways. The book ends by examining potential scenarios for the future of US–Colombian relations.

Notes

1 Schoultz, *Beneath the United States*.

2 Haig, *Caveat*.

3 George Kennan, quoted in Schmitz, *Thank God They're on Our Side*, p. 149.

4 *Miami Herald*, 20 August 2003. <http://www.miami.com/mld/miamiherald/6572125.htm>

5 Alton Frye, *Humanitarian Intervention: Crafting a Workable Doctrine* (Washington, DC: Council on Foreign Relations, 2000).

6 Human Rights Watch, *Colombia's Killer Networks: The Military–Paramilitary Partnership and the United States* (New York: Human Rights Watch, 1996). For up-to-date figures see Human Rights Watch <http://www.hrw.org/americas/colombia.php> and Amnesty International <http://web.amnesty.org/library/eng-col/index>

7 United Nations, Human Development Indicators, Colombia 2003. <http://hdr.undp.org/reports/global/2003/indicator/cty_f_COL.html>

8 Pearce, *Colombia*.

9 Ibid., p. 63.

10 Michael McClintock, *The United States and Operation Condor: Military Doctrine in an Unconventional War*. Paper presented at Latin American Studies Association, Washington, DC, September 2001, p. 28.

11 School of the Americas Watch, *Colombia: 10,000 SOA Graduates*. <http://www.soaw.org/new/docs/Colombia10,000grads.pdf> The School of the

Americas has recently changed its name to the Western Hemispheric Institute for Security Cooperation (WHINSEC), a 'cosmetic' change in the words of one of its supporters, Senator Paul Coverdell. See <http://www.soaw.org> for more details.

12 Richani, *Systems of Violence*, p. 2.

13 Robert Pastor, *Whirlpool: US Foreign Policy Toward Latin America and the Caribbean* (Princeton, NJ: Princeton University Press, 1992), p. 32; for a good overview of the difference between realist and liberal approaches see Michael Doyle, 'Peace, Liberty and Democracy: Realists and Liberals Contest a Legacy', in Cox et al. (eds), *American Democracy Promotion*, pp. 21–40.

14 Richard Downes, *Landpower and Ambiguous Warfare: The Challenge of Colombia in the 21st Century* (US Army War College, Strategic Studies Institute, 1999), p. 5.

15 Passage, *The United States and Colombia*, p. 29.

16 Rabasa and Chalk, *Colombian Labyrinth*.

17 Dennis Rempe, *The Past as Prologue? A History of U.S. CI Policy in Colombia, 1958–66* (US Army War College, Strategic Studies Institute, 2000). <http://www.derechos.net/paulwolf/colombia/prologue.htm>

18 Ibid.

19 Ibid.

20 Center for International Policy, *Paint by Numbers: Trends in US Military Programs with Latin America and Challenges to Oversight*, August 2003, p. 4. <http://www.ciponline.org/colombia/paintbynumbers.pdf>

21 *Washington Times*, 19 July 2002.

22 *Washington Post*, 24 February 2002. <http://www.washingtonpost.com/ac2/wp-dyn?pagename=article&node=&contentId=A57958-2002Feb23>

23 Raphael Perl, 'US–Andean Drug Policy', in Bruce Bagley and William Walker (eds), *Drug Trafficking in the Americas* (Miami: University of Miami Press, 1995), p. 34. My emphasis.

24 Roberto Steiner, 'Hooked on Drugs: Colombian–US Relations', in Victor Bulmer-Thomas and James Dunkerley (eds), *The United States and Latin America: The New Agenda* (Cambridge, MA: Harvard University Press, 1999), p. 171.

25 Ibid., p. 159.

26 Ibid., p. 173. On the weaknesses of US human rights monitoring in Colombia, see my *US Human Rights Monitoring in Colombia*, 30 August 2003. <http://www.colombiajournal.org/colombia166.htm>

27 Sewall H. Menzel, *Cocaine Quagmire: Implementing the U.S. Anti-Drug Policy in the North Andes-Colombia* (Lanham, MA: University Press of America, 2002).

28 Ron Chepesiuk, *Hard Target: The U.S. War against International Drug Trafficking, 1982–1997* (North Carolina: McFarland, 1998).

29 Patrick Clawson and Rensselaer Lee, *The Andean Cocaine Industry* (New York: St Martin's Press, 1998).

30 Drexler, *Colombia and the United States*, p. 167.

31 Bruce Bagley and Juan Tokatlian, 'Dope and Dogma: Explaining the Failure of US-Latin American Drug Policies', in Jonathon Hartlyn, Lars Schoultz

and Augusto Varas (eds), *The United States and Latin America in the 1990s: Beyond the Cold War* (London: University of North Carolina Press, 1992), p. 217.

32 Ibid., p. 221.

33 Crandall, *Driven by Drugs*, p. 7.

34 Russell Crandall, 'Clinton, Bush and Plan Colombia', *Survival*, 44(1), 2002, p. 163; for my critique of Crandall's article and his response, see Doug Stokes, 'Debating Plan Colombia', *Survival*, 44(2), 2002, pp. 183–8.

35 Crandall, *Driven by Drugs*, p. 45.

36 Crandall, 'Clinton, Bush and Plan Colombia', *Survival*, p. 169.

37 Ibid., p. 170.

38 Crandall, *Driven by Drugs*, p. 8.

39 *Guardian*, 4 February 2003. <http://www.guardian.co.uk/colombia/story/0,11502,888496,00.html>

40 Wilkin, 'Revising the Democratic Revolution – into the Americas', pp. 663–4.

41 James Petras, *The Geopolitics of Plan Colombia*, November 2001. <http://www.rebelion.org/petras/english/Petras_on_Plan_Colombia.pdf> p. 3.

42 Giraldo, *Colombia*.

43 Richani, *Systems of Violence*, p. 147.

44 Kirk, *More Terrible than Death*, pp. 241–2.

45 For a sample of Chomsky's work on US policy in Latin America, see Noam Chomsky and Edward Herman, *The Washington Connection and Third World Fascism*; Chomsky, *Year 501*; Noam Chomsky, *Latin America: From Colonization to Globalization* (Boston: South End Press, 1993).

46 Noam Chomsky, *Rogue States: The Rule of Force in World Affairs* (London: Pluto Press, 2000), p. 65.

47 Ibid., p. 73.

48 Noam Chomsky, *Power and Terror: Post-9/11 Talks and Interviews* (New York: Seven Stories Press, 2003), p. 70.

49 Chomsky makes reference to the initial stages of US CI intervention in Colombia, but does not go into any great detail. See Chomsky, *Rogue States*, pp. 70–2.

50 These documents were taken from the US National Archives, and the records of the US Department of State. They were made available between 2000 and 2002. See <http://www.colombiawar.org> for more information.

51 To date no English-language scholarship has made use of these data, and very little mention has been made of them within the popular media. The exception is the BBC. See BBC, 'US "Heading Deeper" in Colombia Conflict', 3 May 2002. <http://news.bbc.co.uk/1/hi/world/americas/1966916.stm>

52 For a selection of my published academic work on US policy in Colombia see 'Why the End of the Cold War Doesn't Matter', pp. 569–85; 'Better Lead than Bread?', pp. 59–78. In relation to US counter-insurgency in El Salvador, see 'Countering the Soviet Threat?', pp. 79–102. For a selection of my non-academic work on Colombia see 'Propaganda and Plan Colombia: Perception

Management of the US's Terror War', *NarcoNews,* 7 June 2002; 'Worthy and Unworthy Victims in Colombia's War of Terror', *Colombia Report,* 24 March 2003; 'La Doctrina Militar Estadounidense y La Guerra del Terror en Colombia', *Soberania,* September 2002.

2 | US objectives in Latin America during the Cold War

Orthodox historical interpretations of US foreign policy have become dominant within IR, and are regularly adopted as unproblematic and uncontested modes of historical analysis by neo-realist, liberal and even more critically inclined IR theorists. Broadly speaking, these orthodox accounts view US Cold War foreign policy as having been reactive to Soviet expansionism, with the USA's primary grand strategy in the developing world being containment of the Soviet Union. US intervention is thus predominantly interpreted as defensive and driven by a bipolar security logic. Counterposed to this interpretation, and yet almost entirely absent from conventional understandings, are revisionist accounts. These argue that US Cold War foreign policy was primarily driven by the desire to construct, defend and extend a liberal capitalist international order while maintaining the US position as the dominant state within that order. Revisionists argue that US interests within the Third World were primarily economic with concomitant strategic and ideological considerations. Specifically, these interests were the maintenance of access to raw materials, the continued flow of capital from the developing world to the developed, access to cheap labour and the destruction of social forces or states that followed a path of development independent of US control.

Orthodox interpretations of US Cold War foreign policy: East versus West

Realist and liberal analysts of US foreign policy tend to view the Cold War in bipolar terms and work with an orthodox historical interpretation of its origins and operation.[1] An orthodox historiography views the Soviet Union as having had expansionist tendencies in the Third World during the Cold War and as fundamentally hostile to Western security. As a consequence US foreign policy within the Third World was driven by a defensive reaction to Soviet expansionism, with the pre-eminent US national interest being Soviet containment.[2] US foreign policy is thus predominantly viewed as a response to Soviet hostility within a bipolar system; US domestic politics play a relatively minor role.[3] In policing and containing threats to global capitalism, George

Kennan, the director of the US State Department's policy planning staff, authored 'The Sources of Soviet Conduct', which provided the policy framework and overriding rationale for the USA's Cold War grand strategy of Soviet containment.[4] The essay articulated a vision of a political war between the USA and what was characterized as the mutually antagonistic communist world. Kennan argued that the USSR's 'brand of fanaticism' was wholly 'unmodified by any of the Anglo-Saxon traditions of compromise' and was 'too fierce and too jealous to envisage any permanent sharing of power'.[5] The main element of US policy towards the Soviet Union 'must be that of a long-term, patient but firm and vigilant containment of Russian expansive tendencies'.[6] US President Harry Truman first publicly wedded the policy of Soviet containment to US foreign objectives in 1947 when he stated: 'One of the primary objectives of the foreign policy of the United States is the creation of conditions in which we and other nations will be able to work out a way of life free from coercion.' The USA was characterized by a 'way of life' which was 'based upon the will of the majority, and is distinguished by free institutions, representative government, free elections, guarantees of individual liberty, freedom of speech and religion, and freedom from political oppression'. Counterposed to these values was the Soviet Union whose political system was 'based upon the will of a minority forcibly imposed upon the majority. It relies upon terror and oppression, a controlled press and radio; fixed elections, and the suppression of personal freedoms.' Throughout the world, Truman argued, it 'must be the policy of the United States to support free peoples who are resisting attempted subjugation by armed minorities or by outside pressures'.[7] Thus the USA's post-war grand strategy became articulated around a vision of Soviet containment.

Kennan argued that the immediate task of US containment after the Second World War was to use economic aid to insulate the shattered Western European capitalist economies from the ideological threat posed by the Soviet Union. Kennan's vision of containment as primarily a political and diplomatic task was increasingly superseded by a militarized containment orientation in the early 1950s.[8] Throughout the 1950s Western Europe and Japan were successfully rebuilt and incorporated within a US-led international capitalist order. Concomitant to this process of incorporation was a gradual shift of US containment efforts from the advanced capitalist countries to the underdeveloped Third World. Factors precipitating this shift included the enforced nuclear peace between the superpowers in Europe and Soviet leader Nikita Khrushchev's declaration of support for the developing world's anti-colonial wars of 'national liberation'. Among US foreign policy planners these new wars of national liberation were characterized as communist insurgencies that had the potential to encroach gradually upon Western spheres of influence.[9] The successful nationalist revolution in Cuba led by Fidel Castro in 1959 added to US fears that communism was on the march in its own backyard. US President John F. Kennedy argued that the 'free world's security can be endangered not only by nuclear attack, but also by being nibbled away at the periphery by forces of subversion, infiltration, intimidation, indirect or non-overt aggression, internal revolution, diplomatic blackmail, guerilla warfare or a series of limited wars'.[10] Indigenous insurgencies were viewed as dangerously threatening to US interests through their ability to be hijacked by communist forces whose 'aggression is more often concealed than open' and who 'in some cases control whole areas of independent nations'.[11] The domino theory provided a succinct visual metaphor for the potential spread of regional pro-Soviet subversion throughout the developing world. It was argued that if this were to happen, US credibility would be weakened in the eyes of its allies, and its resolve to resist Soviet aggression would be questioned.[12]

In resisting and rolling back alleged Soviet aggression in the Third World, the USA sometimes carried out covert warfare and government destabilization. The USA also installed and backed a number of pro-US dictatorships throughout the Third World as a bulwark against what were labelled Soviet-backed insurgencies.[13] Although these regimes' practices were frequently anti-democratic, and they often carried out human rights abuses, these policies were deemed necessary to resist the alleged negative consequences for both US and global security should a pro-Soviet regime assume power. Conservative scholars tend to argue that this was an unfortunate but necessary policy consequence of resisting the global spread of Soviet communism.[14] Liberal scholars tend to argue that sometimes US fears were overstated, and have examined the role that Cold War belief systems have played in exaggerating US perceptions of Soviet expansion in the periphery, the influence that domestic power groups have exerted on US foreign policy, and the effect that bureaucratic rivalry has had upon US foreign policy formation.[15] However, the divergence between realist and liberal opinion over US Cold War policy means within the Third World tends not to extend to divergence over the ends, the USA's innate right to pursue these ends, or the essentially benign character of Cold War US foreign policy.

These orthodox historical interpretations have been employed by conventional IR scholars as if historical debates as to the nature of the Cold War and US foreign policy are largely settled and unproblematic.[16]

This is not the case. Revisionist historiography credibly challenges the basis of orthodox accounts and yet has been occluded in liberal and realist historical analyses of US foreign policy and its role in managing North–South relations during the Cold War. These revisionist arguments provide a number of novel insights. First, they provide a more nuanced account of the underlying reasons for US policy towards the developing world by analysing US policy as guided by economic considerations *as well as* concomitant strategic rationales during the Cold War era. Liberal and realist accounts tend to concentrate on the security dimensions of US foreign policy and characterize US security policy as largely driven by anti-communist containment concerns. In so doing they ignore the role that economic considerations have played in US foreign and security policy and their subsequent role in the construction and maintenance of a capitalist international order. As a result of this widening of the focus to encompass the political economy of US foreign policy, revisionists also provide a novel insight into the nature of perceived threats to US interests in the developing world and the concomitant underlying drives towards US intervention. Revisionists make the argument that the primary threat to US interests during the Cold War came from *any* form of independent development in the Third World and not just from communist forces allegedly linked to the Soviet Union. This is a very interesting theoretical and empirical claim concerning the nature of North–South relations and the role of US policy in retarding socio-economic reforms throughout the developing world largely because IR's conventional wisdom portrays US foreign policy as inherently benign and democratic.

Second, and more importantly for the central argument of this book, these revisionist arguments instantiate a different set of theoretical and empirical insights about the nature of the post-Cold War era. By taking the USA's primary mission during the Cold War as the defence and extension of global capitalism from any threats, including but extending beyond Soviet expansionism, revisionists claim that US post-Cold War policy is characterized by significant continuity with its earlier concerns. That is, US post-Cold War goals continue to be the commitment to the preservation of global capitalism with the USA as the pre-eminent state, and the destruction of social forces that may credibly threaten these relations.

Revisionist historiography and US Cold War foreign policy: North versus South

In the early 1970s, a new form of revisionist history emerged that challenged the prevailing orthodox consensus on the origins of the Cold

War and the operation of US foreign policy. Revisionists accord far less explanatory weight to the alleged anarchic structure of the international system than do either liberal and (neo)-realist IR scholars and instead ground US foreign policy-making within the geo-economic and strategic interests of US (trans)national capital and the construction of a world order conducive for the long-term preservation of capitalism.[17] Hence they work with an understanding of the USA as an empire, and US interests as essentially imperialist in relation to the Third World, and thus reject theoretical understandings of US foreign and security policy that see it as driven by an objective 'national interest' which transcends sectional class-based interests.[18] Gabriel Kolko and Joyce Kolko argue that in the immediate post-war period the USA's aim was to 'restructure the world so that American business could trade, operate, and profit without restrictions everywhere. On this there was absolute unanimity among American leaders, and it was around this core that they elaborated their policies and programs.'[19] Fred Block argues that in the post-war period, 'American policy-makers were more concerned about national capitalism in Western Europe than they were with a possible invasion by the Red Army or successful socialist revolution'. He continues that it is 'necessary to place the Cold War in the context of the American effort to create a certain type of world economy'.[20] Revisionists thus theorize the US state as an essentially imperial capitalist state in relation to the Third World.[21]

James Petras and Morris Morley define the imperial state as 'those executive bodies or agencies within the "government" that are charged with promoting and protecting the expansion of capital across state boundaries by the multinational corporate community headquartered in the imperial center'. The US imperial state exercises both an economic and coercive function, which serve to 'facilitate capital accumulation on a global basis'.[22] US foreign policy is thus institutionally derived through the relation between the US state and US capital in so far as the US state must ensure the generic global conditions for capital accumulation. This structurally derived notion of the US state, and by extension US foreign policy, is not to deny the agency of US state planners but merely to locate agency within the structural and institutional milieu within which US state planners must work. As US Transnational Corporations (TNCs) expand abroad, and a larger share of their profits are derived through international expansion, so the 'activities of the imperial state have become increasingly important for the maintenance of these "building blocks" of U.S. capitalist economy'.[23] Petras and Morley contrast the capitalist state with the imperial state and conclude that the two are different in so far as within the bounds of the nation-state, the capitalist state is 'the only source of sovereign authority', while the imperial state exercises its authority 'in a field of competing and aspiring sovereigns–competing imperialist states, regional powers, and local authorities'.[24] The emergence of the USA as the dominant imperial state within the world system is a relatively recent phenomenon, and was largely spurred on by the collapse of earlier European imperial systems and the emergence of the USA as a global superpower charged with the maintenance of global capitalism in the immediate post-war period.

Petras and Morley argue that throughout the developing world the US imperial state functions through local 'intermediaries linked through military and economic alliances of bilateral ties'. These links 'are sustained through the reciprocal exchanges that mutually benefit the factions of ruling classes in each country' in tandem with a series of socio-cultural linkages. Petras and Morley continue that the 'imperial state project requires the "throwing down" of roots into the *society* to create a social and cultural infrastructure to sustain the otherwise narrow and fragile base of external domination'.[25] US imperial state planners serve to 'mediate the class interests of the ascendant groups within the ruling class in each configuration of forces. As such, they have *discretionary* power in the day-to-day tactical and conjunctural determinations.'[26] Bureaucratic considerations and differences may occur within the imperial state architecture, but this discretionary power operates 'within a larger universe, defined by the organizing principles of the capitalist system'.[27] Within this larger universe, security considerations may sometimes outweigh immediate economic concerns; nevertheless, the management of the welfare of the global capitalist system still confers the absolute boundaries of policy. For example, US coercive intervention within a developing nation may be more financially costly than non-intervention, or there may be little overall US capital penetration within the target country. However, the strategic logic guiding intervention is subordinate to the wider logic of the *global* management of a US-led capitalist system which may be threatened by attempts at independent development within the periphery that may spread to other developing nations.[28] A developing country that attempts to pursue independent development may provide what Oxfam calls the 'threat of a good example'.[29]

The internal planning record provides clear indications as to the way in which the USA constructed its interests in the developing world during the Cold War. As it became increasingly obvious to the allied powers that they would emerge victorious from the Second World War, US planners began to focus on the shape of the new international order. With the bankrupting of Great Britain, the custodian of global capitalism prior to the end of the Second World War, the USA emerged from the war with unrivalled military, political and economic power. In 1942, US Secretary of State Cordell Hull argued that leadership 'towards a new system of international relations in trade and other economic affairs will devolve largely on the United States because of our great economic strength'. He went on to assert that the USA 'should assume this leadership and the responsibility that goes with it, primarily for the reasons of pure national self-interest'.[30] In relation to the developing world, Hull called for 'international investment' so as to make capital 'available for the sound development of latent natural resources and productive capacity'.[31] In this new role, the US national interest was articulated around a dual vision; the maintenance and defence of an international system open to capital penetration, coupled with a concomitant global geo-strategy of containing social forces considered inimical to capitalism, including but extending beyond communism.[32] National Security Council Document 68 (NSC 68) was one of the central documents outlining the USA's policy of containment. Within it, but largely ignored by conventional accounts of US policy, was a very clear statement of intent on the part of the USA. NSC 68 argues that the USA's 'overall policy at the present time' is 'designed to foster a world environment in which the American system can survive and flourish'. NSC 68 went on to assert that even 'if there were no Soviet Union we would face the great problem of the free society … of reconciling order, security … with the requirement of freedom'.[33]

This reconciliation of order, security and freedom and the US role in fashioning world order was encapsulated in the 'Grand Area' concept developed by the influential Council on Foreign Relations and senior US policy-makers, and was used as the blueprint for US policy in constructing the post-war international system.[34] The Grand Area strategy emerged from an analysis of what caused the Second World War: the disintegration of the inter-war international order and the emergence of rival spheres of influence and protectionist blocs. The Grand Area strategy sought to eliminate rival imperialisms and called for the opening up of closed territories for American investors and traders combined with the incorporation of rival capitalist nations under US economic, political and military hegemony.[35] This strategy required the break-up of the old European empires and included not only what had been formerly under British imperial control, but also the Western hemisphere, the Far East and the Middle East.[36] The Third World and its subordination to Western economic and political interests were thus crucial for the functioning of global capitalism. Kennan summarized these objectives in a top secret planning document in 1948, he argued that the USA had 'about 50% of the world's wealth, but only 6.3% of its population … In this situation, we cannot fail to be the object of envy and resentment. Our real task in the coming period is to devise a pattern of relationships that will permit us to maintain this position of disparity.'[37]

The Third World was thus crucial to servicing the needs of the advanced industrial capitalist economies, with US foreign policy geared towards the maintenance of these asymmetric relationships. Soviet expansionism (real, imagined or used as a pretext for intervention) was merely one of a number of threats to the interests of US capitalism within the developing world. The primary threat was indigenous nationalism that threatened to rearticulate national economies to global markets on terms that might not be entirely beneficial for an increasingly transnational capitalist political economy.[38] The US imperial state thus acted to protect the interests of capital through the maintenance of an international system open to capital penetration while destroying social forces that threatened the process of global capital accumulation. This becomes much clearer when examining concrete examples of US intervention.

What was the USA containing in Latin America during the Cold War?

The case of Guatemala The earliest US intervention in Latin America justified as a response to Soviet expansionism was the 1954 US-backed coup in Guatemala that overthrew the democratically elected administration of Jacobo Arbenz. President Eisenhower condemned Arbenz's government as a 'Communist dictatorship' that had been established as an outpost 'on this continent to the detriment of all American nations', while Secretary of State John Dulles stated that, under Arbenz, Guatemalans were living under a 'Communist type of terrorism'.[39] In fact, Arbenz's coalition government was drawn from a wide political spectrum. The communist Guatemalan Labour Party, the smallest party within Arbenz's coalition, had only four of a total of fifty-one seats.[40] Arbenz's government was mildly nationalist and, in the words of a US State Department paper, enjoyed support from a number of groups including 'anti-Communist nationalists in urban areas'.[41] Moreover, the Soviet Union had no diplomatic mission in Guatemala nor did it provide any military assistance.

Prior to Arbenz's election, 2 per cent of Guatemala's population owned 70 per cent of all arable land. Arbenz nationalized and distributed uncultivated land that belonged to the US multinational United Fruit.

The land was given to 100,000 landless peasants. He also instituted social reforms that included the recognition of trade unions and adult literacy campaigns. Crucially, Arbenz did not carry out widescale nationalization of foreign-owned industries, but instead built up nationally-owned industries such as a hydroelectric plant and a large Atlantic port. This strategy was designed to limit the power of foreign companies through direct competition rather than through the nationalization of foreign assets. Arbenz's model of development was thus a nationally-based capitalism with a mixed economy aimed at bolstering local industries.

These domestic reforms were seen as a direct threat to US interests. In 1953, Charles R. Burrows of the US State Department's Bureau of Inter-American Affairs argued that the economic reforms in Guatemala threatened US interests because they provided a potential workable model of development for neighbouring countries that was not wholly open to US capital. He stated: 'Guatemala has become an increasing threat to the stability of Honduras and El Salvador. Its agrarian reform is a powerful propaganda weapon; its broad social program of aiding the workers and peasants in a victorious struggle against the upper classes and large foreign enterprises has a strong appeal to the populations of Central American neighbors where similar conditions prevail.'[42] In response, the USA, along with key US corporations such as United Fruit (which had significant interests in Guatemala and close ties to the Eisenhower administration), financed and armed a number of senior Guatemalan military officers to overthrow the Arbenz government.[43] Recently declassified documents outline the role of the CIA. US assistance to the coup-plotters 'included budgeting, training programs, creation of hit teams, drafting of target lists of persons, and transfer of armaments'.[44] The coup members were drawn from sections of the Guatemalan military unhappy with Arbenz's programme of reform. They subsequently overthrew Arbenz in 1954. Once Arbenz realized that the US-backed coup would succeed, he announced his resignation over national radio. In his speech he declared that the USA had

> used the pretext of anti-communism. The truth is very different. The truth is to be found in the financial interests of the fruit company and the other US monopolies which have invested great amounts of money in Latin America and fear that the example of Guatemala would be followed by other Latin countries ... I was elected by a majority of the people of Guatemala, but I have had to fight under difficult conditions ... I took over the presidency with great faith in the democratic system, in liberty and the possibility of achieving economic independence for

Guatemala. I continue to believe that this program is just. I have not violated my faith in democratic liberties, in the independence of Guatemala and in all the good which is the future of humanity.[45]

The US coup ended democracy in Guatemala and inaugurated forty years of various US-backed dictatorships. The Guatemalan Commission for Historical Clarification was set up as part of the 1994 peace process and was the officially recognized body investigating human rights abuses in Guatemala during the years of dictatorship. The commission concluded that Guatemalan state forces murdered 200,000 people during the 1980s, and 'committed acts of genocide' against Guatemala's Mayan indigenous people.[46] In sum, Arbenz's programme of industrial protectionism for incipient Guatemalan industries coupled with his land reform programme were considered a symbolic threat to US interests through their potential for inspiring other underdeveloped Latin American nations to follow a path of development not entirely under US control.

The case of Cuba The USA feared the threat of independence in Cuba as well. Fidel Castro led Cuba's successful revolution in 1959, overthrowing the US-backed dictator, Fulgencio Batista. US President Kennedy declared that he would not allow a 'communist satellite' that was only 'ninety miles off the coast of Florida'.[47] However, both the internal planning record and the trigger for US hostility illustrate a set of concerns that extend far beyond fears of Soviet expansionism. Kennedy's Special Assistant, Arthur Schlesinger, argued that the problem in Cuba was 'the Castro idea of taking matters into one's own hands' whereby the 'poor and underprivileged, stimulated by the example of the Cuban revolution, are now demanding opportunities for a decent living'. In relation to alleged Soviet expansionism, Schlesinger outlined that the primary threat to US interests was the Soviet Union's alleged 'flourishing [of] large development loans and presenting itself as the model for achieving modernization in a single generation'.[48] Similarly, the CIA told the White House in 1964 that Cuba's experiment in 'statism', that is state interventionism to protect national industries, was bad for US capital: 'the climate for private enterprise has taken a sharply adverse turn ... Cuba's experiment ... and any appearance of success there could have an extensive impact on the statist trend elsewhere in the area.'[49] These concerns with internal reforms that favoured the 'poor and underprivileged' and the US desire to destroy the symbolic threat that Cuba represented is also confirmed by the diplomatic record of early US policy manoeuvring whereby the USA sought to destroy Cuba economically prior to any significant Soviet alignment.[50] The Cuban economy was heavily dependent on its crucial sugar exports to US markets which the USA sought to use as leverage to ameliorate Cuban domestic reforms. As a result of this and Cuba's fear of a cut in its sugar quota, Cuba signed an agreement with the USSR that sought to barter sugar for oil. American-owned oil refineries in Cuba, with US government encouragement, refused to refine Soviet crude oil, a crucial need for the Cuban economy that relied heavily on external energy supplies.[51] In response to this situation, and amid increasing fears of a complete US embargo of sugar purchases, the Cubans nationalized a number of the largest American-owned refineries. This in turn led to a complete suspension of American sugar purchases. The Soviets then offered to make up for this shortfall through increased purchases of the now surplus Cuban sugar crop.[52] In short, the USA sought to destroy economically post-revolutionary Cuba prior to any significant alignment with the Soviets. This was recognized by US planners. Kennedy's Secretary of State, Dean Rusk, outlined the fact that the US embargo would 'deprive Castro of dollar exchange to the extent that he is unable to dispose of approximately $60–70 million annually of these commodities in this market or in other markets with convertible currencies'. This in turn would help to 'deplete his already low foreign exchange position'.[53] It can therefore be concluded that US pressure forced Cuba into a clear alignment with the Soviet Union.

This series of US provocations took place against the backdrop of increased calls for US military intervention in Cuba and an increasingly warlike posture on the part of the new Kennedy administration that culminated in the US-backed paramilitary invasion of Cuba at the 'Bay of Pigs'. Schlesinger feared the impression that the 'Bay of Pigs' invasion would have on world public opinion. He stated that 'many people in the United States and probably most people outside the United States will, unless countermeasures are put into immediate play, see a vast gap between what they regard as the minor threat presented by a tiny nation of 7 million to the great United States and the massive response'. He went on to state that people 'will assume that we are acting, not to protect our safety, but to protect our property and investments'. Moreover, Schlesinger posited the potential for the negative portrayal of US motives as a result of US aggression: 'The objective will be to portray the Soviet Union as the patron and protector of nationalists, Negroes, new nations and peace and to portray the Kennedy Administration as a gang of capitalist imperialists maddened by the loss of profits and driven to aggression and war.' Schlesinger outlined ways of countering this perception by emphasizing key themes. These were 'that Castro is threatened, not by Americans, but by Cubans justly indignant over his betrayal of his own revolution ... that we sympathize with these patriotic Cubans, and ... that there will be no American participation in any military aggression against Castro's Cuba'. He went on to state:

[if] our representatives cannot evade in debate the question whether the CIA has actually helped the Cuban rebels, they will presumably be obliged, in the traditional, pre-U-2 manner, to deny any such CIA activity. (If Castro flies a group of captured Cubans to New York to testify that they were organized and trained by CIA, we will have to be prepared to show that the alleged CIA personnel were errant idealists or soldiers-of-fortune working on their own.)[54]

Even after the failure of the Bay of Pigs to end Castro's government, the CIA continued to argue that Cuba's 'export of physical aid to revolutionary movements, whilst important, is much less significant than the threat posed by Castro's example and general stimulus of these movements'.[55] In 1964 the US State Department summarized Cuba's threat to US interests and stated that 'the primary danger we face in Castro is not what he does in the way of distributing arms, disseminating propaganda, training subversives, and dispatching agents, but in the impact that the very existence of his regime has upon the leftist movements in many Latin American countries'.[56] In sum, the USA feared the potential loss of control that would be engendered by a model of development that appealed to Cuba's 'poor and underprivileged' and, more crucially, presented a symbolic alternative model of development to other Third World nations, especially in Latin America. Washington's hostility towards Cuba, and its planning to overthrow Castro, occurred prior to any significant alignment of Castro's Cuba with the USSR, with US hostility towards Cuba heavily responsible for pushing Cuba into the arms of the USSR. US planners were aware of the negative propaganda that a US invasion would cause and sought themes to counter the portrayal of US policy as a case of 'economic imperialism' by emphasizing the indigenous nature of opposition to Castro's Cuba, and the blanket denial of US involvement, and continued to conclude years after Cuba's Soviet alignment that the primary threat to US interests was Cuba's example to other Latin American nations.[57]

The case of Chile The pattern was similar in Chile. President Salvador Allende was elected in Chile in 1970. Allende was a socialist who sought good relations with the USA. He began a series of social democratic reforms after his election that worried US planners. The internal US planning record indicates clearly that the principal concern for US planners was not whether Chile aligned itself with the Soviet Union, but the symbolic threat that Allende's government presented. For example, in a US national security meeting held on 6 November 1970, US President Richard Nixon claimed that he would refuse to allow Chile to carry out these reforms while still enjoying good relations with the USA. Nixon declared that if 'we let the potential leaders in South America think they can move like Chile and have it both ways, we will be in trouble … No impression should be permitted in Latin America that they can get away with this, that it's safe to go this way.' Nixon stated quite clearly that the potential or actual alignment of Chile with the Soviet Union was of little importance: 'If Allende can make it with Russian and Chinese help, so be it, but we do not want it to be with our help, either real or apparent.' Nixon continued that the 'main concern' for the USA in relation to Allende was that he 'can consolidate himself and the picture projected to the world will be his success'. This was seen as very dangerous as it threatened to give 'courage to others sitting on the fence in Latin America'. Nixon explained how the USA would overthrow Allende: 'I want to work on this and on the military relations, put in more money. On the economic side we want to give him cold turkey. Make sure that the EXIM [Export Import Bank of the United States] and the IOs [International Organizations] toughen up.' US Secretary of State William Rogers added that the US 'military should keep in contact with their Chilean colleagues and try to strengthen our position in Chile'.[58] The USA subsequently supported a coup to unseat Allende. Then CIA director Richard Helms stated that the USA would 'support, by benevolent neutrality at the least and conspiratorial benediction at the most, a military coup which would prevent Allende from taking office'.[59] Allende was overthrown in 1973, and a US-backed dictatorship was installed under General Augusto Pinochet. Allende was murdered within eight hours of the beginning of the coup.[60] In sum, Nixon stated quite explicitly that it did not particularly matter whether Chile received either Russian or Chinese help. Furthermore, the primary threat, as was the case in the other examples examined so far, was the symbolic threat that Chile posed to US hemispheric hegemony. In eliminating this threat, the USA backed a covert destabilization campaign designed to topple the Chilean government. The story is similar in the case of Nicaragua.

The case of Nicaragua When the leftist Nicaraguan Sandinistas overthrew the US-backed dictatorship of Anastasio Somoza in 1979, the World Council of Churches commented that the Sandinistas were 'bent on a great experiment which, though precarious and incomplete at many points, provides hope to the poor sectors of society, improves the conditions of education, literacy and health, and for the first time offers the Nicaraguan people a modicum of justice for all rather than a society offering privilege exclusively to the wealthy ... and to the powerful'.[61]

Nevertheless, US President Ronald Reagan committed the USA to the destruction of the revolution. He declared that 'the security of our own borders depends upon which type of society prevails [in Central America], the imperfect democracy seeking to improve, or the Communist dictatorship seeking to expand'.[62] Reagan linked Nicaragua to Cuba and thus the USSR. However, Cuba had encouraged Nicaragua to maintain strong diplomatic and economic ties to the USA, having realized that 'small states cannot afford the luxury of opposing the United States'.[63] Mexico became Nicaragua's largest backer, with $500 million in credits given by 1984.[64] Western European countries supplied $282.9 million, while multilateral lending institutions such as the United Nations Development Programme (UNDP) and World Bank provided $632.2 million by 1984.[65] A report prepared for the US State Department concluded: 'aid from Western Europe and UN agencies has been ... substantial, and hence crucial. Furthermore, it must also be said that in the context of her overall aid to Third World nations, Moscow's commitment to Nicaragua is modest.'[66] (Eastern bloc aid combined amounted to only 24.2 per cent or $605.6 million by 1984.)

Nicaragua gradually came to rely more on Soviet aid when the USA applied pressure to lending countries and multilateral organizations. For example, the Nicaraguan government sent a loan request to the Inter-American Development Bank (IDB) in 1985 requesting $100 million to develop its private-sector agriculture. Then US Secretary of State George Shultz sent a letter to the bank threatening to withdraw US support for the bank if the loan was made, but gave no reason as to why this would be the case. A senior IDB official later remarked: 'I have never seen such political pressure on the bank as in the last four years.'[67] The blocking of this loan illustrates the hypocrisy of the Reagan administration as the private agricultural sector was the very area that Washington had said it had hoped to preserve against an alleged Marxist takeover. Similarly, Nicaraguan reliance on Soviet-supplied arms did not start until 1982. The Nicaraguans had attempted to secure arms from Western sources for two years after the revolution, even approaching the USA for military aid. The Nicaraguans did manage to secure a $15.8 million deal with France, a deal that US Secretary of State Alexander Haig criticized as a 'stab in the back'. In March 1982, French President François Mitterrand assured Reagan that the delivery of helicopters included in the package would experience indefinite delays.[68] In the face of mounting American hostility, including a US-backed insurgency movement called the Contras, and the diminishing prospects of securing Western arms for self-defence, the Sandinistas increasingly turned to Moscow. Thus, as in the case of Cuba, the USA was instrumental in further cementing Nicaraguan reliance on Soviet arms, which, according to a classified US intelligence report seen by the *Wall Street Journal*, were primarily 'defence orientated' and 'may have been prompted by the escalation of the CIA-backed Contra war'.[69] Mitterrand's assurances to President Reagan came in the same year that the World Health Organization awarded Nicaragua its prize for the 'most significant achievement in public health by a Third World nation' and two years after UNESCO honoured Nicaragua for its 1980 literacy campaign which reduced illiteracy rates among adults from 50 per cent to below 15 per cent.[70] A 1985 Americas Watch report also noted that human rights abuses in Nicaragua by government forces had virtually disappeared (unlike abuses by the US-backed El Salvadoran and Guatemalan governments). The report goes on to note that, in Nicaragua, 'there is no systematic practice of forced disappearances, extrajudicial killings or torture, as has been the case with "friendly" armed forces in El Salvador'.[71]

Soviet policy in Latin America

Since the late 1960s, Soviet policy in Latin America had been conducted with a view to maintaining good diplomatic and economic ties with as many countries as possible. In so doing the Soviets had 'put support for revolution low on its list of priorities',[72] with ideological orientation no guarantee of Soviet support either. For example, in 1979, due to the US grain embargo imposed on the Soviet Union as a result of its invasion of Afghanistan, Soviet reliance on Argentinian grain increased substantially. By 1982 the Soviet Union was taking approximately one-third of Argentina's entire grain crop. During this same period the Argentinian anti-communist junta was carrying out a US-backed 'dirty war' on its own internal opposition that included the outlawing of the pro-Moscow Communist Party. The Soviet Union abstained from votes condemning Argentina within the UN and, crucially, refused to break off any diplomatic or economic ties to the Argentine government. There was thus no guarantee that on ideological grounds alone the USSR would align itself with a leftist government. Furthermore, by 1979 Cuba was costing the USSR $3 billion annually and there is no evidence to suggest that reformist governments would immediately align themselves or subordinate their foreign policy to that of the Soviet Union.[73] Indeed, when one considers the proximity of Latin America to the United States and its reliance on US business and good favour with multilateral lending organizations, coupled with the threat of US-backed sanctions and the very real possibility of covert destabilization or overt invasion, it seems unlikely, to say the least, that any reformist government would seek immediately to align itself with the USSR.

What can we conclude from these examples? First, in the case of Latin America, the orthodox interpretation of US Cold War foreign policy that informs both realist and liberal interpretations is empirically unsustainable as it views US foreign policy as almost solely driven by US security concerns defined as its need to contain Soviet expansionism. US hostility to these states occurred prior to any significant Soviet alignment, and as a result of domestic policies that favoured the poor majorities of those nations. Moreover, the predominant US foreign policy discourse labelled 'communist' any reforms that favoured a nation's poor majorities or lessened reliance on US capital and decreased the levels of expropriated profit while providing an alternative model of national development for other developing nations. Furthermore, and again contrary to the realist and liberal argument, these fears were very clearly articulated by US policy planners and were central to US decisions to intervene and overthrow alternatives to US aligned states. Second, the stated desire to contain Soviet expansion was clearly used as the central pretext for US intervention in Latin America throughout the Cold War period. As illustrated above, however, the internal record reveals a varied set of concerns. The 'Soviet expansionism' thesis, and the equation of reformist domestic policies with international communism, served as a propaganda device with (in the case of Cuba at least) a relatively sophisticated understanding on the part of US planners of the potential negative publicity that unilateral US intervention would produce, and ways to counter the negative portrayal of US policy as economic imperialism. Thus a crucial aspect of US intervention involved the use of threat discourses, and the linking of perceived enemies to alleged existential threats to US national security, which, during the Cold War, became the Soviet Union.[74] Third, in extending and defending a liberal capitalist order, US foreign policy was directly responsible for overthrowing democratically elected governments and installing dictatorships that murdered thousands of their own people. The revisionist perspective, by refuting the notion that these policy measures were necessary to contain Soviet expansionism, thus highlights the enormous human costs associated with the preservation of US interests and the defence of capitalism in Latin America. That is, even if conventional understandings of US policy agree with the notion that alongside the desire to contain Soviet expansionism ran the US objective of extending market relations, the revisionist perspective brings into focus the normative consequences inherent within the USA's extension and defence of capitalist market relations.

Notes

1 See for example, Arthur Schlesinger Jr, 'The Origins of the Cold War', *Foreign Affairs*, 46, 1967, pp. 22–52; Dean Acheson, *Present at the Creation: My Years in the State Department* (New York: W.W. Norton, 1969); Hugh Seton-Watson, *Neither War Nor Peace: The Struggle for Power in the Post-war World* (New York: Praeger, 1960). Although there has emerged a 'post-revisionist' historiography, it has been argued convincingly that post-revisionism acts as a form of 'rearguard' neo-orthodoxy masquerading as a synthesis of both the orthodox and revisionist positions; Bruce Cummings, 'Revising Post-revisionism or, the Poverty of Theory in Diplomatic History', *Diplomatic History*, 17(4), 1993, pp. 539–69. For examples of post-revisionism see John Lewis Gaddis, *The United States and the Origins of the Cold War, 1941–1947* (New York: Columbia University Press, 1972); John Lewis Gaddis, 'The Emerging Post-revisionist Synthesis on the Origins of the Cold War', *Diplomatic History*, 7(3), 1983, pp. 171–204.

2 Lynn Eden, 'The End of US Cold War History? A Review Essay: A Preponderance of Power: National Security, the Truman Administration, and the Cold War, by Melvyn P. Leffler', *International Security*, 18(1), 1993, pp. 174–207.

3 George Kennan, *Realities of American Foreign Policy* (Princeton, NJ: Princeton University Press, 1954); for a good critical overview of international history see Hunter (ed.), *Rethinking the Cold War*.

4 George Kennan, 'The Sources of Soviet Conduct', in George Kennan, *American Diplomacy* (Chicago, IL: University of Chicago Press, 1984), pp. 107–28.

5 Ibid., p. 110.

6 Ibid., p. 119.

7 Harry Truman, *Address before a Joint Session of Congress*, 12 March 1947. <http://www.yale.edu/lawweb/avalon/trudoc.htm>

8 George Kennan, 'Reflections on Containment', in Terry L. Deibel and John Lewis Gaddis (eds), *Containing the Soviet Union: A Critique of US Policy* (Washington, DC: Pergamon-Brassey's, 1987), p. 16.

9 Lawrence Freedman, *Kennedy's Wars: Berlin, Cuba, Laos and Vietnam* (Oxford: Oxford University Press, 2002).

10 John F. Kennedy, 'Defense Policy and the Budget: Message of President Kennedy to Congress, March 28, 1961', in Richard P. Stebbins (ed.), *Documents of American Foreign Relations, 1961* (New York: Harper and Row, 1962), pp. 51–63.

11 John F. Kennedy, 'Special Message Delivered by President Kennedy to Congress on Urgent Special Needs: May 25, 1961', from the *John F. Kennedy Library and Museum* <http://www.cs.umb.edu/jfklibrary/j052561.htm>

12 See Paul H. Nitze, *From Hiroshima to Glasnost: At the Centre of Decision – A Memoir* (London: Weidenfeld and Nicolson, 1989), pp. 214–55.

13 Schmitz, *Thank God They're on Our Side*.

14 For the classic conservative articulation of this perspective, see Kirkpatrick, *Dictatorships and Double Standards*; see also Haig, *Caveat*.

15 Robert Jervis, *Perception and Misperception in International Politics* (Princeton, NJ: Princeton University Press, 1976); Schoultz, *National Security and United States Policy Towards Latin America*; Robert Jervis and Jack Snyder, *Dominoes and Bandwagons: Strategic Beliefs and Great Power Competition in the Eurasian Rimland* (New York: Oxford University Press, 1991).

16 See for example Christopher Layne, 'From Preponderance to Offshore Balancing: America's Future Grand Strategy', *International Security*, 22, 1997, pp. 86–124; John Lewis Gaddis, 'Toward the Post-Cold World', *Foreign Affairs*, 70(2), 1991, pp. 102–22.

17 See Kolko, *The Politics of War*; Patterson, *Meeting the Communist Threat*; Williams, *The Tragedy of American Diplomacy* (New York: Norton, 1988); Walter LaFeber, *Inevitable Revolutions: The United States in Central America* (New York: Norton, 1984).

18 There are a number of different debates as to the nature and definition of imperialism and neo-imperialism with a commonality being the agreement as to the asymmetrical nature of the international system, the transfer of surplus from the periphery to the core capitalist countries and the pervasive nature of the political, economic and military mechanisms to ensure this transfer. For a good introduction to the different definitions of imperialism within the Marxist tradition see Anthony Brewer, *Marxist Theories of Imperialism: A Critical Survey* (London: Routledge, 1980).

19 Kolko and Kolko, *The Limits of Power*, p. 2.

20 Fred L. Block, *The Origins of International Economic Disorder: A Study of United States International Monetary Policy from World War II to the Present* (Berkeley: University of California Press, 1977), p. 10.

21 Nicos Poulantzas, 'The Problem of the Capitalist State', *New Left Review*, 58, 1969, pp. 67–78.

22 James Petras and Morris Morley, 'The U.S. Imperial State', in James Petras, with Morris H. Morley, Peter DeWitt and A. Eugene Havens, *Class, State, and Power in the Third World, with Case Studies on Class Conflict in Latin America* (Montclair, NJ: Allanheld, Osmun, 1981), p. 3.

23 Ibid.

24 Ibid.

25 Ibid., p. 5.

26 Ibid., p. 10.

27 Ibid. There are a number of critical theories on the role of the US state within world capitalism. For a good overview see Barrow, *Critical Theories of the State*.

28 There is an emergent 'global-capitalist' literature that points to the increasing emergence of a nascent transnational state apparatus and transnational class formation with the advent and intensification of the transnationalization

of global capitalism in the early 1970s. This literature critiques conventional accounts of US imperialism as overly committed to a state versus market dichotomy and to nation-statism. See Robinson, *A Theory of Global Capitalism*.

29 Melrose, *Nicaragua*.

30 Cordell Hull quote taken from R. T. Robertson, *The Making of the Modern World: An Introductory History* (London: Zed Books, 1986), p. 113.

31 Cordell Hull quote taken from Kolko, *The Politics of War*, p. 251.

32 See ibid. See also LaFeber, *America, Russia and the Cold War, 1945–1980*; Williams, *History as a Way of Learning*.

33 Paul Nitze, *NSC 68 United States Objectives and Programs for National Security*, 14 April 1949. <http://www.fas.org/irp/offdocs/nsc-hst/nsc-68.htm>

34 The most extensive study of the Council on Foreign Relations and the Grand Area concept is Laurence H. Shoup and William Minter, *Imperial Brain Trust: The Council on Foreign Relations & United States Foreign Policy* (London: Monthly Review Press, 1977); see also Stephen Gill, *American Hegemony and the Trilateral Commission* (Cambridge: Cambridge University Press, 1990).

35 Shoup and Minter, *Imperial Brain Trust*, pp. 117–77. See also Stephen Gill, 'Pax Americana: Multilateralism and the Global Economic Order', in Anthony McGrew (ed.), *Empire* (Milton Keynes: Open University Press, 1994).

36 See Laurence H. Shoup and William Minter, 'Shaping a New World Order: The Council of Foreign Relations: Blueprint For World Hegemony', in Holly Sklar, *Trilateralism: The Trilateral Commission and Elite Planning for World Management* (Boston, MA: South End Press, 1980), pp. 135–56 for an excellent overview of primary data sources and declassified documentation in relation to the Council of Foreign Relations and its role in US foreign policy formation. See also Robinson, *Promoting Polyarchy*, p. 15.

37 Kennan, *Foreign Relations of the United States, 1948*, pp. 524–5.

38 Gabriel Kolko, *The Roots of American Foreign Policy* (Boston, MA: Beacon Press, 1969), p. 79.

39 Quotes in William Blum, *Killing Hope: US Military and CIA Intervention Since World War II* (Maine: Common Courage Press, 1986), p. 73.

40 Manu Saxena, *United Fruit & the CIA*, 17 March 1999. <http://eatthestate.org/03–26/UnitedFruitCIA.htm>

41 US State Department, quoted in Blanche Wiesen Cook, *The Declassified Eisenhower* (New York: Doubleday, 1981), pp. 240–1.

42 Burrows quoted in Gleijeses, *Shattered Hope*, p. 365; see also James F. Siekmeier, '"The Most Generous Assistance." U.S. Economic Aid to Guatemala and Bolivia, 1944–1959', *Journal of American and Canadian Studies*, 11, 1994, p. 26.

43 For more on the role that United Fruit played in the overthrow of Guatemalan democracy, see Schlesinger and Kinzer, *Bitter Fruit*.

44 Kate Doyle and Peter Kornbluh, *CIA and Assassinations: The Guatemala 1954 Documents*. National Security Archive Electronic Briefing Book No. 4. <http://www.gwu.edu/~nsarchiv/NSAEBB/NSAEBB4/>

45 Arbenz quoted in Schlesinger and Kinzer, *Bitter Fruit*, p. 200.

46 The Commission for Historical Clarification, *Guatemala: Memory of*

Silence. <http://shr.aaas.org/guatemala/ceh/report/english/default.html>

47 Speech by President John F. Kennedy on Cuba, 21 September 1960. <http://www.historyofcuba.com/history/baypigs/jfk-1.htm>

48 Arthur Schlesinger, 'Report to the President on Latin American Mission', 10 March 1961, in *Foreign Relations of the United States, 1961–1963*, Vol. XII ('The American Republics') (Washington, DC: US Government Printing Office, 1996), pp. 13–33.

49 CIA, 'Survey of Latin America', 1 April 1964, quoted in Lefeber, *Inevitable Revolutions*, p. 157.

50 Carla Anne Robins, *The Cuban Threat* (Philadelphia, PA: ISHI Publications, 1985), p. 17.

51 Thomas G. Patterson, *Contesting Castro: The United States and the Triumph of the Cuban Revolution* (Oxford: Oxford University Press, 1995).

52 Jutta Weldes, *Constructing National Interests. The United States and the Cuban Missile Crisis* (London: University of Minnesota Press, 1999), pp. 168–9.

53 Dean Rusk, *Memorandum from Secretary of State Rusk to President Kennedy*, 24 February 1961. Kennedy Library, President's Office Files, Countries Series, Cuba, Security, 1961. <http://www.fas.org/irp/ops/policy/docs/frusX/index.html>

54 Arthur Schlesinger, *Memorandum from the President's Special Assistant to President Kennedy*, Washington, 10 April 1961. Kennedy Library, National Security Files, Countries Series, Cuba, General, 1/61–4/61. <http://www.fas.org/irp/ops/policy/docs/frusX/index.html>

55 Central Intelligence Agency, Facts, Estimates and Projections, 2 May 1961, quoted in Piero Gleijeses, *Conflicting Missions: Havana, Washington and Africa 1959–1976* (London: University of North Carolina Press, 2002), p. 16.

56 US Department of State, *Caribbean: Cuba*, 13 February 1964, quoted in Gleijeses, *Conflicting Missions*, p. 16; Gleijeses book is an excellent overview of the development of Cuban foreign policy during the Cold War and its autonomy from the Soviet Union (especially in relation to Cuban intervention in Africa).

57 Recently declassified information points to Castro's desire to initiate good relations with both the Kennedy and Johnson administrations right up to the end of 1964. Lisa Howard, a US newswoman, interviewed Castro in Havana in May 1963. Howard was debriefed by the CIA upon her return to the USA. Her debriefing was read by then US President Kennedy. In it she emphasized Castro's 'interest in better relations with Washington'. After the assassination of Kennedy, Castro sent a further notice of his desire for good relations to the new Johnson administration, which was subsequently ignored. For the full declassified documentation outlining this see Peter Kornbluh, *Kennedy and Castro: The Secret Quest for Accommodation*, National Security Archive Electronic Briefing Book No. 17, 1999. <http://www.gwu.edu/~nsarchiv/NSAEBB/NSAEBB18/index.html>

58 Nixon quote taken from White House, *National Security Meeting on Chile Memorandum of Conversation*, 6 November 1970. <http://www.gwu.edu/~nsarchiv/NSAEBB/NSAEBB8/nsaebb8.htm>

59 Richard Helms, 'Genesis of Project FUBELT', Washington, Central Intelligence Agency, 16 September 1970. <http://www.gwu.edu/~nsarchiv/NSAEBB/NSAEBB8/ch03–01.htm>

60 Robinson Rojas Sandford, *The Murder of Allende* (New York: Harper and Row, 1976).

61 World Council of Churches, 'Report on Nicaragua', 1983, quoted in Melrose, *Nicaragua*, p. 12.

62 Ronald Reagan, *Radio Address to the Nation on Central America*, 24 March 1984. <http://www.reagan.utexas.edu/resource/speeches/1984/32484a.htm>

63 Carla Anne Robins, 'Examining the "Cuban Threat"', in Abraham F. Loenthal and Samuel F. Wells, Jr (eds), *The Central American Crisis: Policy Perspectives* (Washington, DC: Wilson Center, 1985), p. 110.

64 Robert Armstrong, Marc Edelman and Robert Matthews, 'Sandinista Foreign Policy: Strategies for Survival', *NACLA Report on the Americas*, May/June 1985, p. 36.

65 Ibid., p. 51.

66 Report prepared by Carl G. Jacobsen for the US Department of State, *The Jacobsen Report: Soviet Attitudes Towards, Aid to, and Contact with Central American Revolutionaries*, June 1984, p. 21.

67 John Lamperti, *What are we Afraid of? An Assessment of the 'Communist Threat' in Central America* (Boston, MA: South End Press, 1988), p. 29.

68 On the Sandinista search for arms, see George Black and Robert Matthews, 'Arms from the USSR – or from Nobody', *The Nation*, 31 August 1985, p. 148; on Mitterrand's assurances to the USA, see Armstrong et al., 'Sandinista Foreign Policy', p. 19.

69 *Wall Street Journal*, 3 April 1985.

70 Thomas W. Walker, *Nicaragua: The First Five Years* (New York: Praeger, 1985), pp. 14–16.

71 Americas Watch, *Report on Human Rights in Nicaragua* (New York: Americas Watch, 1985), p. 3; for an analysis of the USA's use of CI in El Salvador during the 1980s so as to destroy alternative development models see my (2003) 'Countering the Soviet Threat?'

72 Jonathon Steele, *Soviet Power: The Kremlin's Foreign Policy – Brezhnev to Chernenko* (New York: Simon and Schuster, 1984), p. 168; see also Piero Gleijeses, *Conflicting Missions, Havana, Washington and Africa 1959–1976* (London: University of North Carolina Press, 2002).

73 On the unlikelihood of a subordination of leftist states' foreign policies to the Soviet Union, see Morton H. Halperin, 'US interests in Central America: Designing a Minimax Strategy', in Lowenthal and Wells (eds), *The Central American Crisis*, p. 25.

74 For more on threat discourses and their role in US foreign policy, see Simon Dalby, *Creating the Second Cold War: The Discourse of Politics* (London: Frances Pinter, 1990).

3 | US objectives in Latin America after the Cold War

While conventional understandings of US foreign and security policy work with an orthodox interpretation of US foreign policy during the Cold War, the post-Cold War period has led to a shift in analyses that seek to chart the purported new orientations of US post-Cold War foreign policy.[1] Given the presumptions of conventional realist and liberal IR scholars, it is logical that in the absence of the Soviet Union they would view US foreign policy as characterized by change from its Cold War orientation of Soviet containment. This new post-Cold War discontinuity thesis presumes, or takes as given, that US foreign policy objectives in the post-Cold War era have in some way significantly changed, especially in relation to the Third World. This thesis extends beyond IR scholarship into the popular discourses of US policy-makers themselves and the international institutions that manage world order. Counterposed to this discontinuty thesis stands a *continuity thesis* which argues that US post-Cold War foreign policy is characterized by significant continuity in its objectives in relation to the developing world. The primary US goals continue to be the promotion and defence of a liberal international order with the USA as the pre-eminent hegemonic capitalist state, and the continued opposition to reformist states and movements that threaten this order.[2] This is illustrated clearly by the way in which the USA has continued to oppose reformist democracies in Venezuela and Brazil. The orthodox historical interpretation of US Cold War foreign policy and discontinuity arguments in relation to US post-Cold War foreign policy are, at least in relation to Latin America, unsustainable. Furthermore, the discontinuity interpretations treat the analysis of US foreign policy as if the debates over its motivations, drives and consequences are unproblematic and settled.

US post-Cold War foreign and security policy objectives: the discontinuity thesis

With the end of the Cold War a discontinuity thesis has emerged in relation to international relations in general, and US foreign policy more specifically. This thesis emphasizes the primacy of containment of the Soviet Union on US foreign policy during the Cold War, and argues that US objectives in the post-Cold War period are characterized by discontinuity in relation to the Third World. As Joffe has argued: 'During the Forty Years War, also known as the Cold War, America's grand strategy was both elegant and efficient. It consisted of one word: "containment." And its purpose was the break-up or mellowing of Soviet power. Having achieved both objectives, the United States was left without a grand strategy.'[3]

Even structural realists such as Kenneth Waltz, who emphasizes the post-Cold War continuities within international politics, still work with an orthodox interpretation of US Cold War foreign policy that sees it as driven by fears of Soviet expansionism. For example, Waltz argues that for 'almost half a century, the constancy of the Soviet threat produced a constancy of American policy' and with the 'disappearance of the Soviet Union, the United States no longer faces a major threat to its security'.[4] In the face of this apparent post-Cold War dissolution of the USA's grand strategy of containment, Barry Posen and Andrew Ross pose a number of questions that US planners must face in the post-Cold War era: 'what are US interests; what are the threats to those interests; what are the appropriate remedies for threats? In short, what is to be the new grand strategy of the United States?'[5] They outline a number of potential new post-Cold War US foreign policy grand strategies that range from a stance of neo-isolationism that seeks US withdrawal from regional conflict altogether to a grand strategy of primacy which seeks confidently to assert a unilateralist US hegemony.

More pessimistically-inclined discontinuity analysts tend to view the post-Cold War world as potentially more dangerous for US interests. Some of the supposed new threats to US interests include increased inter-capitalist competition, the emergence of expansionist and belligerent developing world ethnic nationalisms and new and more deadly forms of 'post-modern' identity warfare.[6] John Mearsheimer argues that the system of bipolarity had an ordering effect on world politics with an increased potentiality for new political tensions emerging in the post-bipolar era.[7] Samuel Huntington argues that the post-Cold War era will see a reconfiguration of the world along civilizational 'fault lines' that pit the West against new enemies. He argues that these fault lines 'will be the battle lines of the future' with a 'clash of civilizations' dominating relations between the West and the developing world and US foreign policy having to adapt to these new threats accordingly.[8]

More optimistically-inclined interpretations of the post-Cold War period have emphasized the end of ideological struggle with the collapse of the Soviet Union and the global triumph of liberal capitalism.[9] These approaches tend to be aligned quite closely with (neo)-liberal theorists of US foreign policy who stress the pacific potential of liberal capitalism and see the promotion of neo-liberal forms of governance as the best way of ameliorating conflict within an anarchic international system. As such, the promotion of liberal democracy within US foreign policy has been linked to the opportunities presented to US foreign policy-makers by the end of the Cold War. Ikenberry, for example, argues that although US foreign policy has allegedly had a longstanding commitment to exporting a Wilsonian liberalism premised on human rights, democracy and free trade, the end of the Cold War provided a great opportunity to pursue these liberal objectives more stridently. Ikenberry berates the pessimistic discontinuity arguments and argues that for 'all the talk about drift and confusion in American foreign policy, the United States is seized by a robust and distinctive grand strategy' of post-Cold War liberalism.[10] In a similar vein, Tony Smith has argued against the realist presumption that the promotion of human rights and democracy should take second place to US self-interest in international relations. Smith argues that a 'national security liberalism' that supports 'human rights and the establishment of democratic governments abroad' combined with US self-interest (defined as 'the enhancement of American influence in the world') may 'actually serve one another far more often and importantly than most commentators on the US role in world affairs generally suppose'.[11] In place of containment, Smith calls for a post-Cold War US grand strategy to promote democracy and human rights through the enlargement of democratic governments throughout the world.[12] The democratic peace thesis within International Relations has been crucial in theorizing this alleged new orientation within US foreign policy.

The democratic peace thesis has proposed a taxonomy of world order between what is characterized as the Zone of Peace and the Zone of War. This binary taxonomy has come to dominate post-Cold War discussions of developed and developing world relations and the role of US foreign policy within the world order. The Clinton administration enthusiastically adopted the democratic peace thesis as one of its intellectual cornerstones.[13] The thesis argues that inter-state relations between democracies within the Zone of Peace are governed by a Kantian peace while relations within the Zone of War are characterized by a Hobbesian struggle for survival and balance of power politics. The democratic peace posits a causal relationship between the existence of democracy and the absence of inter-state war. Democratic peace proponents ground their arguments on analyses that purport to show the absence of inter-state wars among democracies since 1815, and the essentially pacific nature of their international relations with each other.[14] The absence of war among liberal democracies and the existence of a democratic peace are considered to be 'the closest thing we have to an empirical law in the study of international relations'.[15] Bruce Russett, one of the central democratic peace theorists, has argued that the end of the Cold War destroyed the 'old bases for evaluating the character of international relations' with the 'end of ideological hostility' representing a 'surrender to the force of Western values of economic and especially political freedom'. The existence of a democratic peace among market democracies and the implications of this for world politics are said to be so profound that any discussion of the 'future of international relations' must address this issue.[16] Democracy promotion has thus become one of the central justifications for the conduct of US post-Cold War foreign policy in the developing world, with a number of US-led interventions justified as necessary either to protect democracy or to bring it about. As Michel Feher argues, US and Western European leaders 'proudly associated the end of the Cold War with the advent of an increasingly cohesive international community' that was committed to 'fostering democracy and preventing human rights violations, even when the latter were perpetrated by the agents of a recognized state against their own population'.[17] As such, a number of post-Cold War US interventions, for example the US-led intervention in Kosovo, have been justified as necessary both to promote democracy and end human rights abuses.[18]

This alleged commitment to human rights and democracy has also led to calls for a more robust and ethically-orientated Western military policy of humanitarian intervention to stem human rights abuses in the Third World. Mary Kaldor, for example, has outlined what she calls post-Cold War 'new wars'.[19] These are distinct from earlier, large-scale wars in that they resemble what have traditionally been termed civil wars or low-intensity conflicts. For Kaldor, these categories are insufficient because they work with a notion of sovereignty that fails to grasp fully the increasingly globalized complexities of new wars, and the subsequent dissolution of distinctions between the internal and external, state and non-state nature of new wars.[20] She explicitly relates the 'new war' model to the 'globalisation of the 1980s and 1990s' and the ending of the Cold War that 'contributed in important ways to the new wars'.[21] She calls for transnational institutions and Western liberal democracies to underwrite and enforce a global cosmopolitan peace. Underlying this call for a more strident post-Cold War policy of Western military humanitarian intervention has been the call for the deepening of market relations that are seen to have pacific effects. As Ikenberry claims 'trade and economic openness have liberalizing political impacts' with the view that 'free trade and open markets strengthen society and create zones of autonomy that limit the reach of the state' sitting 'at the core of American foreign policy efforts'.[22] Thus, calls for the spread of democratic governance are inherently linked to the deepening of capitalist market relations.

This equation between democracy, pacific governance and the end of the Cold War is echoed by US policy-makers and international institutions. In the words of the Commission on Global Governance, the end of the Cold War has 'created a unique opportunity for strengthening global co-operation to meet the challenge of securing peace, achieving sustainable development, and universalising democracy'.[23] The extension of a democratic peace through the spread of market-led globalization has formed a cornerstone of post-Cold War US foreign policy. Former Secretary of State James Baker argued that with the end of the Cold War we 'now have a chance to forge a democratic peace' with 'real democracies', not going to 'war with each other'.[24] Anthony Lake, US President Bill Clinton's National Security Adviser, explicitly linked democracy promotion in the developing world to the USA's post-Cold War grand strategy by arguing that the 'successor to a doctrine of containment must be a strategy of enlargement – enlargement of the world's free community of market democracies'. He continued that during the Cold War 'even children understood America's security mission; as they looked at those maps on their schoolroom walls, they knew we were trying to contain the creeping expansion of that big, red blob. Today ... we might visualize our security mission as promoting the enlargement of the "blue areas" of market democracies.' US foreign policy, however, is pacific and does 'not seek to expand the reach of our institutions by force, subversion or repression'.[25] Clinton stated that the best way to guarantee democracy in the developing world was through the spread of globalization which, he argued, leads to a 'world without walls' and an 'explosion of democracy'[26] and provides 'more of our own people – and billions around the world – the chance to work and live and raise their families with dignity'.[27] US post-Cold War foreign policy has thus been very clearly linked to the promotion of liberal democracy and the intensification of neo-liberal globalization within the Third World.

Echoing Smith's calls for a national security liberalism, this deepening of capitalist social relations and democracy has also been linked to US security interests. In the words of Clinton's *National Security Strategy of Engagement and Enlargement*, 'democratic states are less likely to threaten our interests and more likely to co-operate with the United States to meet security threats and promote free trade; the more that democracy and political and economic liberalization take hold in the world the safer our nation is likely to be and the more our people are likely to prosper'.[28] Current US President George W. Bush stated that the USA 'must have a great and guiding goal' which is to 'turn this time of American influence into generations of democratic peace'.[29] Furthermore, globalization represents the 'triumph of human liberty across national borders' and provides the opportunity for the USA 'to prove that freedom can work not just in the new world or old world, but in the whole world'.[30] The principal mechanisms for the spread of democracy and neo-liberal governance within the developing world have been the use of international institutions such as the IMF which has conditionally linked its loans to market reforms. These forms of global governance are said to be leading to the replacement of an anarchic international system with what McGrew characterizes as a set of 'pluralistic arrangements by which states, international organisations, international regimes, non-governmental organisations, citizen movements and markets combine to regulate or govern aspects of global affairs'.[31] Michel Camdessus, the former International Monetary Fund's (IMF) director, stated that: 'ours is the first generation in history that finds itself in the position of being called upon to influence global affairs – not from a position of military conquest or imperial power, but through voluntary international cooperation'.[32] Alongside these international institutions and global forms of governance has been the use of Western military force in what are characterized as humanitarian interventions within the Third World to prevent human rights abuses and topple dictatorships.

The events of September 11 have served to shift this foreign policy commitment to democracy promotion, human rights and multilateralism to a more unilateral and militarized focus on North–South relations. Unrest and insufficiently pro-US states within the Third World are increasingly seen as dangerously threatening to US security through their potential linkages to international terrorism. For example, in his State of the Union Address, President Bush constituted an 'axis of evil' made up of a series of allegedly rogue states that were potentially 'catastrophic' for US security.[33] Accompanying this policy shift from a multilateralist approach to world order, a number of commentators have called for the establishment of a new US empire to safeguard US security. Thomas Friedman compares the events of September 11 to the Second World War and the end of the Cold War in terms of its significance for international order and US foreign policy: 'World War I gave birth to the League of

Nations and an attempt to re-create a balance of power in Europe, which proved unstable. World War II gave birth to the United Nations, NATO, the IMF and the bipolar US–Soviet power structure, which proved to be quite stable until the end of the Cold War. Now, Sept. 11 has set off World War III, and it, too, is defining a new international order.' Friedman adopts the taxonomy of the democratic peace debates and argues that the new post-September 11 era 'is also bipolar, but instead of being divided between East and West it is divided between the World of Order and the World of Disorder' with the mission of the world of order to 'stabilize and lift up the World of Disorder'.[34] Condoleezza Rice, President Bush's National Security Adviser, affirmed Friedman's point when she declared that 'the collapse of the Soviet Union and 9/11' signified a major shift in 'international politics' with the post-September 11 era providing the USA with the opportunity to 'expand the number of democratic states'.[35] September 11 has thus come to be seen as a defining moment whereby the USA must implement its alleged goals of democracy, human rights and counter-terrorism more forcefully within the developing world. Accompanying this more unilateralist orientation in US foreign policy have been calls for the establishment of a US empire as the best means for achieving US policy objectives. Charles Krauthammer explained: 'People are now coming out of the closet on the word "empire" ... The fact is no country has been as dominant culturally, economically, technologically, and militarily in the history of the world since the Roman Empire.'[36]

Within this new imperial discourse, the USA is seen as a reluctant empire that has inherited the capacity for global power projection due to the preponderance of power left over from the superpower confrontation. Furthermore, the extension and consolidation of its empire in the post-September 11 era is still allegedly driven by defensive considerations to civilize and bring order to what continue to be characterized as zones of war within the developing world. Sebastian Mallaby argues that in the post-September 11 era, 'anti-imperialist restraint' on the part of the USA, which has characterized its foreign policy since 'World War II', is increasingly becoming 'harder to sustain'. He continues that to protect the USA against 'terrorists, drug smugglers and other international criminals' that find refuge in 'failed states', the USA must now acknowledge its 'reluctantly' imperial role in world order, and self-consciously adopt a 'logic of neo-imperialism' when dealing with Third World failed states.[37] Robert Kaplan explained that there is 'a positive side to empire ... It's in some ways the most benign form of order' as a globally hegemonic USA provides the best hope there is for peace and stability.[38] American power projection and consolidation of empire are viewed as the best guarantors for US stability and the protection of US interests, with the alleged lack of American power projection interpreted as the reason for the September 11 attacks. The *Wall Street Journal*'s features editor, Max Boot, argued: 'the Sept. 11 attack was a result of insufficient American involvement and ambition; the solution is to be more expansive in our goals and more assertive in their implementation ... US imperialism – a liberal and humanitarian imperialism, to be sure, but imperialism all the same – appears to have paid off in the Balkans.' He continued, the solution for 'troubled lands' in the developing world is a 'sort of enlightened foreign administration once provided by self-confident Englishmen in jodhpurs and pith helmets'.[39] According to Stratfor, one of the USA's leading intelligence firms: 'Sept. 11 created an unintended momentum in U.S. foreign policy that has led directly to empire-building ... The United States ... is an imperial power, not in the simplistic Leninist sense of seeking markets, but in the classical sense of being unable to secure its safety without controlling others.'[40] September 11 has thus led to calls for a new US empire, with a benign form of imperialism throughout the developing world seen as the best guarantor for US security in the twenty-first century. As I now go on to show, these discontinuity analyses that purport to examine the new orientations and objectives of US foreign policy in the post-Cold War and now post-September 11 era continue to ignore revisionist accounts of US Cold War foreign policy and its underlying drives.

US post-Cold War foreign policy: the continuity thesis

Post-Cold War discontinuity IR scholarship has a presentist bias that occludes the significant continuities in US post-Cold War objectives in relation to the Third World. This extends to the alleged novelty of the supposed *new* imperial relations and can be best explained by the avoid-ance of the analytical concept of imperialism by mainstream IR scholar-ship to explain the long-term relations between the North and South. Fred Halliday contends that while 'IR has recognised the importance of structures of power and inequality' it has treated these structures as 'self-standing entities, separate from, or at best contingently related to, the world market and the global organisation of production'.[41] As we saw above, however, revisionist understandings of US foreign policy provide a useful corrective to conventional understandings through their examination of US intervention within the Third World, and its role in destroying challenges to the capitalist global organization of production. Revisionist understandings of US foreign policy also stand in contradiction to those discontinuity analysts who argue that US post-Cold War foreign policy objectives have significantly changed or that we are now witnessing a new and benign US empire engendered by the events of September 11. The discontinuity arguments outlined above emphasize or presuppose the significantly altered and changed nature of the post-Cold War and post-September 11 eras. This in turn has led to the overestimation of the significance of the Cold War as determinative of global order and US foreign policy between 1945 to 1990 and leads to an overemphasis on the significance of the end of the Cold War for international relations. Revisionist perspectives, in contrast, emphasize the continuities within the post-Cold War era by arguing that the overriding objectives of US policy in the Third World have largely remained unchanged. These objectives continue to be the preservation and defence of a (neo)-liberal international order and the destruction of social forces or states considered inimical to this order. The alleged discontinuities in US objectives, such as democracy promotion and the promotion of human rights, are in fact shifts in the rationales of US foreign policy that mask this deeper and more significant structural continuity in North–South relations. As Michael Cox argues: 'many of the broader objectives sought by the United States since 1989 actually bear a strong resemblance to those it pursued before the end of the Cold War and the fall of the USSR ... the underlying aim of the US, to create an environment in which democratic capitalism can flourish in a world in which the US still remains the dominant actor, has not significantly altered'.[42]

The accuracy of both the discontinuity and continuity arguments can best be examined by looking at the USA's stance towards democratic states and the role that US-led neo-liberal globalization plays in allegedly fostering pacific forms of governance and global wealth creation. In this way we can shift from the rhetoric of US planners to an examination of what US policy actually does. In the next section of this chapter I show that the existence of democracy in Latin America continues to be contingent on the preservation of open economies and social orders deemed unthreatening to US interests and that the USA maintains a number of policy options to contain democracy. These include capitalism (the use of International Financial Institutions, IFIs, and negotiated free trade agreements to tie down national states' policies), coups (the con-tinued and credible threat to revert to authoritarian forms of governance should social forces threaten US interests), and counter-insurgency (the continued funding of counter-insurgency campaigns to destroy armed groups and pacify civil societies).

Transnational capital exercises a profound disciplining power upon the policies pursued by democratically elected governments throughout Latin America. US foreign policy has been instrumental in implementing neo-liberalism both through its multilateral agreements with Latin American states and its domination of the international institutions that are implementing forms of neo-liberal governance throughout Latin America. The Free Trade of the Americas Act (FTAA) builds upon the North American Free Trade Agreement (NAFTA) passed by the US Congress, Canada and Mexico in 1993. NAFTA sought to integrate the economies of North America, Canada and Mexico into a single trading bloc, to dismantle trade barriers, to privatize state-owned industries and to loosen the restrictions on the movement of capital.[43] Like NAFTA, the FTAA seeks to link the economies of all the Latin American nations (with the exception of Cuba) into a single trade bloc. The FTAA is based on a corporate-led model of development that will accelerate post-Cold War neo-liberal reforms of national economies throughout Latin America. It also contains a number of provisions that will strengthen the power of US capital due to the domination of the US economy in the region. The gross domestic product (GDP) of North, Central and South America was $11,000 billion in 2000. However, the USA's share of this GDP was 75.7 per cent, with Brazil, which was the next largest, at 6.7 per cent, Canada's was 5.3 per cent while Mexico's was 3.9 per cent. The other thirty-one nations comprised only 8.4 per cent. Per capita GDP in the USA was $30,600 in 2000 while the lowest, Haiti, stood with just $460.[44] The FTAA will serve to deepen the already overwhelming power of US capital by dismantling national trade barriers to allow easier penetration by US capital and US-subsidized exports, the increase in the privatization (and consequent foreign ownership) of state-owned industries, and the more rigorous enforcement of the intellectual property rights of (mainly) US corporations.[45] The FTAA also has deep implications for democracy in Latin America. For example, the US Trade Representative's office (USTR) has supported 'investor-state' provisions within the FTAA that grant transnational corporations the legal status that had formerly been used for states and provide transnational corporations the ability to use FTAA trade agreements to challenge national laws in court.[46] Thus, if democratically elected governments pursue policies that are deemed harmful to the interests of transnational corporations, those governments can be sued. For example, under the rules of NAFTA, Canada is being sued by the US chemical producer Crompton Corporation, because Canada had responded to health fears over Crompton's pesticide Lindane, and had banned its use on food crops. Crompton is now in the process of suing the Canadian government for $100 million for loss of profits.[47] Even the threat of legal sanctions provides a powerful disciplining force on democratic reforms. That is, states will think twice about instituting social or economic policies that could potentially threaten the interests of transnational corporations if it means that they could be sued for millions of dollars.

The FTAA also provides more liquidity for transnational capital through the lessening of restraints on international capital movements, with the FTAA ensuring the rights of investors to move capital from one nation to the next with no legal impediment. This threat of 'capital flight' also serves to condition the bounds of the democratically permissible within states through the threat of the devaluation of national currencies should policies that may be passed by national governments threaten corporate interests. The conditions attached to loans by the US-dominated transnational institutions such as the IMF and the World Bank have been used to push US foreign policy and economic priorities. For example, the IMF has recently announced that its loans to developing nations would now be conditionally linked to whether or not a state is aligned with the USA's new 'war on terror'.[48]

The disciplining power of largely US transnational capital on democracy and the role of neo-liberalism in strengthening this power are illustrated clearly in the case of Brazil. Luiz Inacio da Silva (Lula) who heads the Brazilian Workers' Party was elected President in October 2002. He has pledged Brazil to a new social-democratic policy that favours Brazil's poor majority. Lula declared that his party 'can guarantee an agrarian reform and that people can eat three times a day'.[49] However, prior to his election, IFIs and banks had attempted to undermine Lula's chances of victory. In May 2002, Merrill Lynch, Morgan Stanley and ABN Amro had issued warnings to investors that caused a run on Brazil's currency, the real. In June, Moody's rating agency altered Brazil's rating from stable to negative. This in turn led to the plummeting of Brazil's currency, which lost 23 per cent of its value between January and June 2002. As 90 per cent of Brazil's foreign debt is linked to the dollar, Brazil's debts increased substantially with a potential default of $250 billion if the real continued to plummet.[50] Largely due to the size of the Brazilian economy, and the exposure of a number of US transnationals in Brazil, the IMF provided a loan of $30 billion to Lula's predecessor, Fernando Henrique Cardoso.[51] This loan was conditional upon the continued implementation of neo-liberal reforms with $6 billion given to Cardoso and the rest saved over for Lula. US Under-Secretary of the Treasury, Kenneth Dam, argued that the USA 'supported the August decision to provide an expanded IMF lending package to Brazil because of confidence in the current policy mix and the firm belief that the short-term liquidity pressures facing Brazil can be alleviated through continuity of such policies'. He went on to outline how IMF conditionality had been linked to the continuation of neo-liberalism in Brazil: 'To ensure that the large majority of IMF resources are provided only if sound policies are observed, the program "backloads" the funds. That is, Brazil will get the majority of the IMF loan only if it adheres to sound policies such as maintaining fiscal prudence and taking concrete steps to reform major impediments to growth such as the current tax code.'[52] Lula's Workers' Party has had to continue the implementation of IMF reforms and has cut government spending. The principal beneficiary of the loan will be two US banks, Citibank and Fleet Boston (with estimates of up to $20 billion of the $30 billion loan being used to service Brazil's debts to these two institutions).[53] The choice in Brazil, then, is quite clear: either follow policies laid down by the IMF that help to service the debt of US banks, or face destabilization of the economy through capital flight, negative credit ratings and the cut-off of 'backloaded' loans. Nevertheless, the use of IFIs to constrain state policies is one of the less overtly coercive mechanisms that can be used to contain democracy in Latin America.

The recent case of the US-backed military coup against the democratically elected government of Hugo Chavez in Venezuela shows the precarious nature of even relatively wealthy democracies within the developing world when attempting to follow an independent foreign policy and modest internal reforms.[54] Venezuela has the largest petroleum reserves outside the Middle East and is one of the USA's largest oil suppliers.[55] Chavez has consistently sought to use Venezuelan leadership within the Organization of Petroleum Exporting Countries (OPEC) to strengthen its bargaining power with Western countries. He has also expressed sympathy for anti-government forces in Ecuador, Bolivia and Colombia, states all loyal to Washington, and is instituting a social-democratic model that seeks to use Venezuela's mineral wealth for its poor majority.[56] Peter Romero, the former State Department Assistant Secretary of State for the Western Hemisphere, called Chavez and his Foreign Minister, Jose Rangel, 'professional agitators'.[57] The current US Secretary of State, Colin Powell, expressed his frustration with Chavez and stated: 'We have not been happy with some of the comments he has made with respect to the campaign against terrorism. He hasn't been as supportive as he might have been.'[58]

The USA backed a coup attempt against Chavez on 11 April 2002.

Immediately afterwards State Department spokesperson Phillip Reeker stated that the USA wished 'to express our solidarity with the Venezuelan people and look forward to working with all democratic forces in Venezuela'. He went on to explain that the coup had been caused by Chavez's 'undemocratic actions' that 'provoked' the 'crisis in Venezuela'.[59] Contrary to this assertion, Chavez had won elections in 1998 and 2000 by the largest majority in four decades of Venezuelan history, and had passed a new democratic constitution by popular referendum in 1999.[60] In backing the coup the US government's National Endowment for Democracy had channelled 'hundreds of thousands of dollars in grants to US and Venezuelan groups opposed to Mr Chavez, including the labour group whose protests sparked off the coup', while the US navy was alleged to have coordinated and aided the coup plotters.[61] Thomas Dawson, the IMF External Relations Director, stated that the IMF stood ready to assist the new junta 'in whatever manner they find suitable'.[62] A Bush administration spokesman stated quite bluntly that although Chavez was 'democratically elected', one had to bear in mind that 'legitimacy is something that is conferred not just by a majority of the voters'.[63] Once Chavez had been returned to power after mass street demonstrations by Venezuela's poor, Miguel Bustamante-Madriz, a member of Chavez's cabinet, argued: 'America can't let us stay in power. We are the exception to the new globalization order. If we succeed, we are an example to all the Americas.'[64] As we can see, the use of a coup to unseat a democratically elected government continues to form an element of the USA's post-Cold War policy within Latin America.

However, the most striking form of policy continuity remains the continued US funding of Latin American military forces despite their atrocious human rights records. For example, throughout the Cold War the principal form of US coercive statecraft was the use of counter-insurgency to destroy social forces considered potentially inimical to US interests. Counter-insurgency was thus used to police the liberal international order instituted throughout Latin America, and formed the principal coercive modality to allegedly 'contain Soviet expansionism' during the Cold War. Even though the Cold War has ended, the USA continues to maintain global links with the majority of Third World militaries through US foreign military aid and training.[65] Throughout the Third World, indigenous US-backed militaries still hold considerable power, and frequently play an instrumental role in direct repression. In the late 1990s the USA was training up to '100,000 foreign soldiers annually' with the training taking place in 'at least 150 institutions within the U.S. and in 180 countries around the world'.[66] US training and aid have increased considerably as part of its new global 'war on terror'. Furthermore, this aid continues to go to states whose military forces are consistently responsible for gross violations of human rights.[67] Latin America is no exception. For example, Chile, Guatemala and Nicaragua received over $350 million in US military aid between 1990–2001.[68] Of all the different forms of US intervention in Latin America, US military aid to repressive militaries is the area most implicated in human rights violations and the containment of democracy. This is largely due to the legacy of US training and aid during the Cold War period which saw the orientation of Latin American militaries towards an internal security role. In Guatemala alone, Amnesty International noted that in 1996 'judges, lawyers, journalists, [and] members of human rights organizations – are frequent victims of torture, extrajudicial executions, abductions and death threats by agents linked to the states' security forces'.[69] What can we conclude from US post-Cold War policy in Latin America?

Contrary to the claims made by discontinuity theorists, US post-Cold War policy continues to be opposed to democracies that pursue policies considered inimical to US interests. The USA can thus be said both to be promoting democracy in so far as it complements US interests and to be containing democracy when those interests are threatened. As I have shown, this was the case in a number of countries during the Cold War, and in the examples examined above continues to be the case in the post-Cold War era. If progressive democratically elected governments threaten to initiate significant socio-economic reforms then a series of policy options are available to US planners to stymie this process. In the case of Brazil, the threat of international capital flight and the conditionalities linked to IMF loans serve to constrain significant moves towards popular reform, with neo-liberalism increasing the anti-democratic power of transnational capital. In the case of Venezuela, the more blunt instrument of a military coup was used in an attempt to end Chavez's democratically elected government. Thus, regardless of the fact that the bipolar competition has ended, there has been a striking continuity in US goals in relation to particular kinds of social forces in Latin America. This is remarkable precisely because US Cold War foreign policy was invariably justified as driven by the very feature of the international system (the Cold War competition) that has ended. I have argued that the best way to account for this continuity is the fact that the US state has long acted in the interests of an increasingly transnationalized set of capitalist interests that predate the end of the Cold War.[70]

In the next two chapters I examine in depth the role of US policy in Colombia both during and after the Cold War. I develop the theme of continuity outlined in this chapter, and show that while there has been a shift in the discourses used to justify US intervention in Colombia, US post-Cold War objectives have remained consistent with its earlier Cold War objectives.

Notes

1 See, for example, Ethan B. Kapstein and Michael Mastanduno (eds), *Unipolar Politics: Realism and State Strategies After the Cold War* (New York: Columbia University Press, 1999); Brown et al. (eds), *America's Strategic Choices*. There are fewer mainstream IR theorists and analysts who examine continuities between the Cold War and post-Cold War period, e.g. Kenneth N. Waltz, 'The Emerging Structure of International Politics', *International Security*, 18(2), 1993, pp. 44–79; Colin Gray, 'Clausewitz Rules, OK? The Future is the Past – With GPS', *Review of International Studies*, 25, 1999, pp. 161–82. However, they still accept as unproblematic the contestable claim that US foreign policy is essentially benign and was defensively driven during the Cold War.

2 By reformist I mean democracies that institute policies that favour the poor majorities of their nations rather than a minority elite and transnational corporations.

3 Josef Joffe, 'Bismarck of Britain. Toward an American Grand Strategy After Bipolarity', *International Security*, 19(4), 1995, p. 94.

4 Kenneth Waltz, 'Structural Realism After the Cold War', *International Security*, 25(1), 2000, pp. 28–9.

5 Barry R. Posen and Andrew L. Ross, 'Competing US Grand Strategies', in Robert J. Lieber (ed.), *Eagle Adrift: American Foreign Policy at the End of the Century* (New York: Longman, 1997), pp. 101–34.

6 Samuel Huntington, 'America's Changing Strategic Interests', *Survival*, 23(1), 1991, pp. 3–17; Stanley Hoffmann, *World Disorders: Troubled Peace in the Post-Cold War* Era (New York: Rowman and Littlefield, 2000); John Mearsheimer and Robert A. Pape, 'The Answer: A Partition Plan for Bosnia', *New Republic*, 14 June 1993; Mary Kaldor, *New and Old Wars: Organized Violence in a Global Era* (Cambridge: Cambridge University Press, 1999).

7 Robert Skidelsky, *The World After Communism: A Polemic for Our Times* (London: Macmillan, 1995); John Mearsheimer, 'Back to the Future: Instability in Europe After the Cold War', *International Security*, 15, 1990, pp. 5–56.

8 Samuel P. Huntington, 'The Clash of Civilizations?', *Foreign Affairs*, 72(3), 1993, pp. 22–49.

9 Francis Fukuyama, *The End of History and the Last Man* (London: Penguin, 1992).

10 G. John Ikenberry, 'America's Liberal Grand Strategy: Democracy and National Security in the Post-War Era', in Cox et al. (eds), *American Democracy Promotion*, p. 104.

11 Tony Smith, 'National Security Liberalism and American Foreign Policy', in ibid., p. 85.

12 Cf. Fareed Samaria, 'The Delusion of Impartial Intervention', *Foreign Affairs*, 76(6), 1997, pp. 22–43.

13 Nicholas Guyatt, *Another American Century? The United States and the World After 2000* (London: Zed Books, 2000), p. 179.

14 See Michael Doyle, 'Kant, Liberal Legacies, and Foreign Affairs', in Michael E. Brown, Sean M. Lynn-Jones and Steven E. Miller (eds), *Debating the Democratic Peace: An International Security Reader* (London: MIT Press, 1996), pp. 3–57; Bruce Russett, 'The Fact of Democratic Peace', in ibid., pp. 58–81. For an excellent set of critical interpretations of the democratic peace thesis see Laffey and Barkawi, *Democracy, Liberalism and War*; Mark Laffey and Tarak Barkawi, 'The Imperial Peace: Democracy, Force, and Globalization', *European Journal of International Relations*, 5(4), 1999, pp. 403–34.

15 Jack S. Levy, 'Domestic Politics and War', in Robert I. Rotberg and Theodore K. Rabb, *The Origin and Prevention of Major Wars* (New York: Cambridge University Press, 1989), p. 88.

16 Bruce Russett, 'The Fact of Democratic Peace', in Brown et al. (eds), *Debating the Democratic Peace*, pp. 58–81.

17 Michel Feher, *Powerless by Design: The Age of the International Community* (Durham, NC: Duke University Press, 2000), p. 32.

18 Robert C. DiPrizio, *Armed Humanitarians: U.S. Interventions from Northern Iraq to Kosovo* (Baltimore, MD: Johns Hopkins University Press, 2002); cf. Noam Chomsky, *The New Military Humanism* (Monroe, ME: Common Courage Press, 1999).

19 Kaldor, *New and Old Wars*.

20 Ibid., pp. 1–3.

21 Ibid., p. 4.

22 Ikenberry, 'America's Liberal Grand Strategy', pp. 114–15.

23 Commission on Global Governance, *How the Commission was Formed.* <http://www.cgg.ch.TheCommission.htm>

24 James Baker quotes taken from Bruce Russett, *Grasping the Democratic Peace: Principles for a Post-Cold War World* (Princeton, NJ: Princeton University Press, 1993), pp. 128–9.

25 Anthony Lake, *From Containment to Enlargement*, 1993. <http://highered.mcgraw-hill.com/olc/dl/35282/14_1_lake.html>

26 Bill Clinton quoted in 'Bill Clinton Comes to Cal', 29 January 2002. <http://www.berkeley.edu-news-features-2002-clinton>

27 Bill Clinton, *Text of Farewell Address*, 19 January 2001. <http://news.bbc.co.uk-hi-english-world-americas-newsid_1125000-1125290.stm>

28 White House, *National Security Strategy of Engagement and Enlargement*, February 1996, pp. 2–7.

29 George W. Bush, *President Bush on Foreign Affairs*, US Department of State International Information Programs, n.d. <http://usinfo.state.gov-products-pubs-presbush-foraf.htm>

30 George W. Bush, *Radio Address by the President to the Nation*, 21 July 2001. <http://www.whitehouse.gov-news-releases-2001-07-20010721.html>

31 Andrew McGrew, 'Democracy Beyond Borders', in David Held and Anthony McGrew (eds), *The Global Transformations Reader: An Introduction to the*

Globalisation Debate (Cambridge: Polity Press, 2000), p. 408.

32 Michel Camdessus quoted in the Canadian Institute of International Affairs, 'The 2000 National Foreign Policy Conference'. <http://www.ciia.org-weekes.htm>

33 George W. Bush, *State of the Union Address*, 29 January 2002. <http://www.whitehouse.gov/news/releases/2002/01/20020129-11.html>

34 *New York Times*, 17 February 2003.

35 Condoleezza Rice, *Remarks by National Security Adviser on Terrorism and Foreign Policy*, 29 April 2002; cf. Jack Snyder, 'Imperial Temptations', *The National Interest*, 71, 2003, pp. 29–40.

36 *The New York Times*, 1 April 2002. <http://www.iht.com-articles-53141.html>

37 Sebastian Mallaby, 'The Reluctant Imperialist: Terrorism, Failed States, and the Case for American Empire', *Foreign Affairs*, 81(2), 2002, pp. 2–7.

38 Kaplan quote in Emily Eakin, *New York Times*, 31 March 2002.

39 Max Boot, 'The Case for American Empire, the Most Realistic Response to Terrorism is for America to Embrace Its Imperial Role', *Weekly Standard*, 15 October 2002. <http://www.weeklystandard.com-content-public-articles-000-000-000-318qpvmc.asp> For an extended discussion of Boot's call for US neo-imperialism see his *The Savage Wars of Peace: Small Wars and the Rise of American Power* (New York: Basic Books, 2002).

40 Author unknown, 'The American Empire', *Stratfor*, 27 June 2002. <http://www.stratfor.biz-lStory.neo>

41 Fred Halliday, 'The Pertinence of Imperialism', in Rupert and Smith (eds), *Historical Materialism and Globalization*, p. 77.

42 Cox, *US Foreign Policy After the Cold War*, p. 5.

43 Public Citizen, *A Ten-Point Plan to Fight for the Americas: No to FTAA*. <http://www.citizen.org/trade/ftaa/TAKE_ACTION_/articles.cfm?ID=8483>

44 *Le Monde Diplomatique*, April 2001.

45 Claudio Katz, 'Free Trade Area of the Americas. NAFTA Marches South', *NACLA: Report on the Americas*, 4 February 2002, pp. 27–31.

46 See William Greider, 'Sovereign Corporations', *The Nation*, 12 April 2001. <http://www.thenation.com/doc.mhtml?i=20010430&s=greider>

47 *Natural Life Magazine*, January 2003. <http://www.life.ca/nl/83/lindane.html>

48 See 'IMF Marries Lending Policy to U.S. Anti-Terrorism Goals', *Stratfor*, 30 April 2002. <http://www.stratfor.com-premium-analysis_view.php?ID=204311>

49 Lula quoted in Bill Vann, 'Brazil's Lula Celebrates Victory, IMF Demands More Austerity', *World Socialist Web Site*, 29 October 2002. <http://www.wsws.org/articles/2002/oct2002/lula-o29_prn.shtml>

50 'Brazil's New Economic Team and Its Conflicting Objectives', *Stratfor*, 20 December 2002. <http://www.stratfor.biz/Story.neo?storyId=208548&countryId=16>

51 *Financial Times*, 22 October 2002.

52 Kenneth W. Dam, *Promoting Growth Throughout the Americas*, *Miami Herald*'s Sixth Annual Conference on the Americas, 15 October 2002.

53 Conn Hallinan, *Backyard Bully?*, Interhemispheric Resource Center, 12 September 2002. <http://www.americaspolicy.org/commentary/2002/0209bully_body.html> See also Jane Bussey, *Miami Herald*, 20 October 2002. <http://www.miami.com/mld/miamiherald/4319370.htm?template=content Modules/printstory.jsp>

54 *Guardian*, 13 May 2002.

55 *Houston Chronicle*, 20 August 2000.

56 *New York Times*, 28 December 2000.

57 *El Pais*, 11 February 2001.

58 Colin Powell, *Testimony to the Senate Foreign Relations Committee*, 5 February 2002.

59 Phillip Reeker, *State Department on Change of Government in Venezuela*, 12 April 2002. <http://usinfo.state.gov/regional/ar/venezuela/02041250.html>

60 On Chavez and his popular democratic mandate see *NarcoNews*, 20 February 2002; on US media responses to the coup see Fairness & Accuracy in Reporting, 'US Papers Hail Venezuelan Coup as Pro-Democracy Move', 18 April 2002. <http://www.fair.org/press-releases/venezuela-editorials.html>; for a good overall context to the background of the coup see Conn Hallinan, 'US Shadow Over Venezuela', *Foreign Policy in Focus*, 17 April 2002. <http://www.fpif.org/commentary/2002/0204venezuela2_body.html>

61 *Guardian*, 29 April 2002.

62 Thomas C. Dawson, *Transcript of a Press Briefing*, International Monetary Fund, 12 April 2002. <http://www.imf.org-external-np-tr-2002-tr020412.htm>

63 *Observer*, 21 April 2002.

64 *New Internationalist*, 29 June 2002.

65 For more detail, especially in relation to US military aid and training in the Third World post 9/11 see Jim Lobe, 'Pentagon Moving Swiftly to Become "Globocop"', *Foreign Policy in Focus*, 12 June 2003. <http://www.fpif.org/commentary/2003/0306globocop.html>

66 Lora Lumpe, *U.S. Foreign Military Training: Global Reach, Global Power, and Oversight Issues*, May 2002. <http://www.foreignpolicy-infocus.org-papers-miltrain-index_body.html>

67 For detailed information on human rights in Latin America see the Human Rights Watch webpage: <http://www.hrw.org/americas/index.php>

68 Federation of American Scientists, *U.S. Arms Transfers Database Search*, n.d. <http://www.fas.org/asmp/profiles/sales_db.htm>

69 Amnesty International, *Amnesty International Appeals on Behalf of Human Rights Defenders in Central American and Mexico*, 10 December 1996 <http://web.amnesty.org/ai> See <http://www.fas.org/asmp/profiles/worldfms.html> for precise details of US training and aid.

70. For more on the transnationalization of capitalism, especially in relation to Latin America, see Robinson, *Transnational Conflicts*.

4 | Installing state terror in Colombia

Throughout the Cold War, Latin America saw the greatest number of US interventions justified under the rubric of anti-communist containment.[1] However, US intervention was designed to roll back forms of progressive social change, with anti-communism providing both a ideological slant and a propaganda pretext for US policy. Throughout the Cold War the principal means for US coercive statecraft in Latin America was CI warfare designed to internally police US-backed dictatorships and to prevent credible challenges to pro-US governments. CI was officially codified and formally used as a central part of US coercive statecraft with President Kennedy's authorization of the 1961 Foreign Assistance Act which sent US aid to developing states to increase bilateral military ties and encourage capitalist-orientated economic development. CI envisaged a broad spectrum of US engagement which encompassed both economic development reforms in host countries and the strengthening of recipient militaries for an internal security role.[2] Walt Rostow, one of Kennedy's National Security Advisers, helped to develop modernization theory as a theoretical component of US-sponsored CI. It theorized the developmental process as a series of stages eventually leading to industrial capitalism, with Third World societies most susceptible to revolution when economies begin to 'take off' towards modernity. Rostow argued that strong internal security arrangements were necessary to insulate the development process from popular reforms during this crucial takeoff period.[3] David Bell, then director of the USA's Agency for International Development (AID), argued that a 'general theory of economic development' requires a 'minimum degree of personal security' with (among others) the Cuban revolution teaching the USA that 'we must often make special adaptations to achieve this' as 'guerrilla warfare and terrorism' are 'obstacles to the peaceful concentration on the problem of economic growth'.[4] However, the economic component of US CI took a back seat to the internal security role of recipient militaries largely due to the resistance of Latin America's indigenous conservative elites to the proposed economic reforms envisaged within CI strategy. These reforms would have required indigenous elites to forgo some of their privileges, which in turn would have impacted upon their economic interests.[5]

The USA's Foreign Assistance Act of 1961 committed the US to improve 'the ability of friendly countries and international organizations to deter or, if necessary, defeat [Communist] aggression'. To this end the USA facilitated 'arrangements for individual and collective security' and assisted 'friendly countries to maintain internal security and stability in the developing friendly countries essential to their more rapid social, economic, and political progress'.[6] In resisting what was characterized as communist expansionism throughout Latin America, US CI doctrine envisaged a war that was to be fought on ideological, political and military fronts. The internal security role of recipient militaries required the policing of their own populations to prevent indigenous social forces from challenging a status quo geared towards what were perceived to be core US interests: the maintenance of pro-US governments and national economies open to US capital penetration.[7] Internally-orientated Latin American national security states wedded to a CI strategy thus formed the bedrock of US policy throughout the Cold War in Latin America. US support took a number of forms, including extensive security assistance, the legitimization of the repressive Latin American states through US contact and the training of Latin American military personnel in a number of US training academies. For example, the US Army training academy for Latin America, then called the School of the Americas (SOA), had trained over 40,000 Latin American military personnel by the end of the Cold War.[8] In 1947, US Secretary of War Robert P. Patterson explained the rationale for the setting up of these academies and the ideological function that they performed: '[T]he provision of United States equipment is the keystone since United States methods of training and organization must inevitably follow its adoption along with far-reaching concomitant benefits of permanent United States military missions and the continued flow of Latin American officers through our service schools. Thus will our ideals and way of life be nurtured in Latin America, to the eventual exclusion of totalitarian and other foreign ideologies.'[9]

As part of the planning process, strong, authoritarian states were seen as the best guarantor of US interests in Latin America. These states, however, frequently carried out mass violations of human rights. US policy was thus at odds with its *publicly* declared aim of preventing human rights abuses and helping incipient democracies to protect themselves from 'communist subversion' during the painful process of development. The USA was linked to human rights abuses not only by installing and supporting allied states, but also through the very doctrines and practices passed on through US CI doctrine.

The internal security role within US-sponsored counter-insurgency not only called for indigenous militaries to confront their armed insurgencies but also, and more crucially, called for the policing and disciplining of various sections of unarmed civil society. In this section I examine a broad CI discourse that was developed by US CI trainers and reinforced throughout the Cold War by continuous US military aid and training. Gearoid O Tuathail and John Agnew define discourses as 'sets of socio-cultural resources used by people in the construction of meaning about their world and their activities', and it is in this sense that I use the term.[10] As I go on to show, the CI discourse served to delegitimate particular social identities while legitimating sets of established institutions and practices.[11]

While the Colombian state was repressive prior to US CI aid and training, the qualitative character of US intervention in Colombia served further to legitimate, support and entrench the strategy of state terrorism. US-sponsored CI was thus directly responsible for the ideological legitimation of widespread state terror directed specifically at civil society in the name of anti-communism. This in turn served to raise the associated costs of dissent and, as I go on to show, was designed to pacify or destroy restive sections of society while insulating national economic and political structures from popular reforms. Within the CI discourse, US policy was thus justified as a necessary response to the bipolar conflict: indigenous insurgencies were portrayed as manifestations of externally sponsored subversion, and guerrilla forces as Soviet proxies. However, within the CI discourse, subversion was defined so broadly that unarmed progressive social forces were linked to subversion through the equation of their social identities with communism. As we shall see, membership of trades unions, political lobbying and even criticism of the government were considered signs of 'communist subversion'. The development of the CI discourse and its institutional links to US training and aid are illustrated most clearly through an examination of the training manuals used by the USA to train local military forces. These manuals give an insight into the CI doctrines that the USA developed and subsequently imparted to the thousands of Latin American military personnel trained during the Cold War period. They also provide an insight into the discursive worldview of US trainers and give clear indications of the kinds of ideological practices inherent in US training of Latin American military forces.

US CI strategy and the legitimation of state terrorism

US Special Forces were the lead agency tasked with the training of indigenous CI military and paramilitary forces: 'The Special Action Force

[US Special Forces] ... provides advisory personnel and mobile training teams to advise, train and provide operational assistance for paramilitary forces.'[12] A 1962 special warfare manual outlined the training programme for the USA's allied security forces. Training included 'guerrilla warfare, propaganda, subversion, intelligence and counter-intelligence, terrorist activities, civic action, and conventional combat operations'.[13] Another Special Forces manual entitled *Counter-Insurgency Operations*, which was used to train recipient militaries, underlined the necessity for US trainers to stress offensive action: 'Stress maintenance of the initiative by prompt offensive actions, economy of force and employment of suitably organized and trained troops and police in all-weather field operations utilizing guerrilla/terrorist tactics.' Within CI warfare, the manual continued, the strategies employed by a recipient state could be broken down into eight key areas. These were 'a) Meeting engagements; b) Attacks; c) Defense; d) Ambushes ... ; e) Raids; f) Pursuit actions; g) Interception actions; h) Terror Operations'.[14] One of the tactics employed as part of the overall CI effort was the use of psychological warfare. A US Army manual, *Psychological Operations*, stated that psychological operations formed a central component of the USA's Cold War CI arsenal: 'Although most past experience by the [US] military in the conduct of propaganda campaigns has been limited to periods of general war or limited war, the realities of the Cold War indicate that military psychological operations has a major and essential mission to fulfill in activities not involving full-scale hostilities.' The manual continued that the primary target 'for tactical psychological operations is the local civilian population'. After other means have failed, pro-US forces can legitimately target civilians to instil terror:

> Civilians in the operational area may be supporting their own government or collaborating with an enemy occupation force. Themes and appeals disseminated to this group will vary accordingly, but the psychological objectives will be the same as those for the enemy military. An isolation program designed to instill doubt and fear may be carried out ... If these programs fail, it may become necessary to take more aggressive action in the form of harsh treatment or even abductions. The abduction and harsh treatment of key enemy civilians can weaken the collaborators' belief in the strength and power of their military forces.[15]

Another manual, entitled *Handling Sources*, continued along similar lines and advocated the harsh treatment of civilians. The manual was used to teach CI forces the art of cultivating government informants within alleged insurgent organizations. The manual states that good techniques to force people to inform were the targeting of family members and the use of physical violence. The 'CI agent could cause the arrest of the employee's parents, imprison the employee or give him a beating as part of the placement plan of said employee in the guerrilla organization'. The manual went on to outline how crucial successful informants are, with an informant's worth increasing through the number of 'arrests, executions, or pacification[s]' the informant's information led to, all the while 'taking care not to expose the employee as the information source'. According to the manual even children were to be used as potential information sources: 'Children are, at least, very observant and can provide precise information about things they have seen and heard, if they are interrogated in the appropriate manner.'[16] The use of state terror was thus overtly advocated as a legitimate technique to be employed by CI forces, with recipient militaries trained in the use of terrorism, and the 'abduction and harsh treatment' of civilians advocated so as to raise the associated costs of dissent. This particular form of terror was used extensively throughout Latin America by US-backed CI forces, and became known by the generic term of civilian 'disappearances' by both the families of the victims and the human rights groups that regularly monitored these forms of coercive statecraft.[17] The Federation of Associations for Relatives of the Detained and Disappeared, which monitors disappearances in Latin America, confirmed the effectiveness of the 'abduction and harsh treatment' in spreading terror among the target population. They argue that the 'objective of forced disappearance is not simply the victim's capture and subsequent maltreatment, which often occurs in the absence of legal guarantees. Because of the anonymity of the captors, and subsequent impunity, it also creates a state of uncertainty and terror both in the family of the victim and in society as a whole.'[18]

One of the key features of the US-backed Latin American states was the institutionalization of torture against perceived enemies with torture practised routinely and on a wide scale by US-backed CI forces.[19] The use of coercive techniques as part of the overall CI effort was advocated by US trainers, and physical and mental coercion were openly advocated as a legitimate part of the counter-insurgent's arsenal. For example, in the CIA's *Human Resource Exploitation Training Manual*, it was stated that although US trainers 'do not stress the use of coercive techniques, we do want to make you aware of them and the proper way to use them'. The manual outlines a number of coercive techniques including sensory deprivation, solitary confinement and different forms of physical torture including bizarre forms of water torture whereby subjects were 'suspended in water and wore black-out masks'. The manual continues: 'stress and anxiety become unbearable for most subjects ... how much they are able to stand depends upon the psychological characteristics of the individual ... the "questioner" can take advantage of this relationship by assuming a benevolent role'. The manual cautions that if a 'subject refuses to comply once a threat has been made, it must be carried out. If it is not carried out then subsequent threats will also prove ineffective.' The training manual concludes that 'there are a few non-coercive techniques which can be used to induce regression, but to a lesser degree than can be obtained with coercive techniques'.[20]

This manual was based on a 1963 manual used by the CIA, the *KUBARK Counterintelligence Interrogation Manual*. Its introduction states that if bodily harm or 'medical, chemical or electrical methods or materials are to be used to induce acquiescence', then prior approval from CIA headquarters is required. The manual continues that if 'a new safehouse is to be used as the interrogation site, it should be studied carefully to be sure that the total environment can be manipulated as desired. For example, the electric current should be known in advance, so that transformers or other modifying devices will be on hand if needed.'[21] The *Baltimore Sun* conducted an investigation into the use of these manuals. They were told by an intelligence source that the 'CIA has acknowledged privately and informally in the past that this referred to the application of electric shocks to interrogation suspects'.[22] In sum, torture was condoned as part of the strategic arsenal available to CI forces in combating alleged subversion. Importantly, torture not only provided an efficient means for inducing 'regression' but also acted to instil terror within target populations.

Aside from the attribution of clandestine state violence to insurgent forces, and the covert use of torture, the principal mechanism employed so as to allow a state plausible deniability was the development and deployment of paramilitary forces.[23] Paramilitary forces provided plausible deniability due to the clandestine nature of their composition, which allowed for a distancing between 'official' state policy and the 'unofficial' use of terrorism directed against civilian populations. Such terror techniques included mass civilian displacement, the pacification of rural populations and the murder of civilians deemed inimical to the overall CI effort (union leaders, human rights workers, teachers and so on). Leaders of paramilitary forces were invariably drawn from sections of a state's security personnel and members from wider society who were seen to have a greater stake in the status quo. A US directive in relation to US CI efforts in Vietnam, which formed the model for US CI in Latin America,[24] explained that paramilitary forces should be specifically drawn from 'the young elite which exists everywhere; those who have a stake in the community' and who wish to 'get ahead in business, professions or politics'.[25] The use of paramilitary warfare was typically characterized by US trainers as a reactive form of counter-terror within US CI doctrine because of the perceived need to fight fire with fire. For example, a 1966 CI manual stated that CI forces 'may not employ mass counter-terror (as opposed to selective counter-terror) against the civilian population i.e., genocide is not an alternative'.[26] This use of terror was doctrinally justified as a necessary response to the alleged terrorism committed by insurgent forces. For example, a 1963 manual argues: 'The methods used by communist-dominated insurgency forces are designed to gain control of the people and to weaken the government and its forces ... Their methods include subversion, infiltration of the government, sabotage and violence ... terrorism by assassination, bombing, arson, armed robbery, kidnapping, torture, and mutilation.'[27]

In practice, however, the 'counter-terror' operations conducted by recipient military and paramilitary forces led to the large-scale abuse of human rights throughout Latin America. Moreover, US trainers and manuals actively called for the strategy of terrorism as a legitimate part of the counter-insurgents' arsenal and bolstered repressive militaries while granting the measures they adopted a degree of strategic legitimacy due to the alleged necessities imposed by the bipolar competition. Perhaps the most damaging aspect of US policy, however, was the marriage between these forms of coercive statecraft and the generic designation of whole swathes of civil societies as inherently inimical and subversive. That is, while a number of the Latin American states had long used repressive measures against their civilian populations, US military aid and training extended beyond arms transfer and numerous training programmes to encompass ideological aspects that sought to portray civil societies themselves as inherently subversive and therefore legitimate battlegrounds for the overall CI effort. For example, the US Army manual entitled *Stability Operations* was translated into Spanish and was used by the School of the Americas to train thousands of Latin American military officers in CI intelligence-gathering.[28] The manual begins by outlining the fundamentally subversive nature of insurgency and its alleged link to the bipolar confrontation:

Recent history has been characterized by the frequent occurrences of insurgencies which have usually taken place in developing and/or emerging nations as a result of having obtained independent status from a colonial power. Frequently, such insurgencies have been Communist inspired or have become subversive in nature as Communist elements manage to gain control of the movement for their own purposes ... In recent years the Communists have instigated or supported insurgencies in many parts of the world as a means of expanding their sphere of influence and/or control.[29]

The manual moves on to outline the centrality of civilian populations to any insurgent movement: 'To succeed in his phased development the insurgent relies on the population as the major source for expansion and replacement of his military forces.' It then extends its definition of subversion beyond *armed* insurgents and explicitly links civil society organizations to the problem of insurgency. For example, it asks, '[a]re there any legal political organizations which may be a front for insurgent activities?' and then highlights the education system as vulnerable to subversion: 'Is the public education system vulnerable to infiltration by insurgent agents? What is the influence of politics on teachers, textbooks, and students, conversely, what influence does the education system exercise on politics?' What 'is the nature of the labor organizations; what relationship exists between these organizations, the government, and the insurgents?' In outlining targets for CI intelligence operations, the manual identifies a number of different occupational categories and generic social identities. These include 'merchants' and 'bar owners and bar girls' and 'ordinary citizens who are typical members of organizations or associations which represent predominant local occupations, such as farming, industry, labor unions, farm cooperatives, social organizations, political parties, religious groups, and other organizations which play an important role in the local society'. In particular, CI forces were to concentrate on '[l]eaders of Dissident groups (minorities, religious sects, labor unions, political factions) who may be able to identify insurgent personnel, their methods of operation, and local agencies the insurgents hope to exploit'. In an overt indication of the equation of labour movements with subversion, the manual then goes on to state that insurgent forces typically try to work with labour unions and union leaders so as to determine 'the principal causes of discontent which can best be exploited to overthrow the established government [and] recruit loyal supporters'. Alongside the designation of certain sectors of the workforce as potentially subversive is the blanket labelling of any moves towards democratic reform or criticism of the status quo as inherently subversive. The US CI discourse thus identified patterns of behaviour and specific types of political activity as fundamentally linked to insurgent activity. For example, the manual states that organizations that stress 'immediate social, political, or economic reform may be an indication that the insurgents have gained a significant degree of control'. It then moves on to detail a series of what it terms 'Insurgent Activity Indicators', which were generic behavioural signs that, allegedly, indicated communist subversion. These indicators were taken as definite signs of subversion: 'Anything that insurgents can do to influence and direct a society toward revolution will be reflected by some overt occurrence or indication, no matter how subtle the action … through recognition of them [the] first clues to insurgent existence and evidence of the growth of the insurgent movement are obtained.' These alleged indications included:

> Refusal of peasants to pay rent, taxes, or loan payments or unusual difficulty in their collection. Increase in the number of entertainers with a political message. Discrediting the judicial system and police organizations. Characterization of the armed forces as the enemy of the people. Appearance of questionable doctrine in the educational system. Appearance of many new members in established organizations such as labor organizations. Increased unrest among laborers. Increased student activity against the government and its police, or against minority groups, foreigners and the like. An increased number of articles or advertisements in newspapers criticizing the government. Strikes or work stoppages called to protest government actions. Increase of petitions demanding government redress of grievances. Proliferation of slogans pinpointing specific grievances. Initiation of letterwriting campaigns to newspapers and government officials deploring undesirable conditions and blaming individuals in power.[30]

Thus, the CI discourse was very specific about the types of democratic lobbying seen to be linked to communism. The quote illustrates clearly that activities considered indications of insurgent subversion were actually practices otherwise considered normal elements of the democratic process within liberal democracies themselves, including in the USA. Indeed, one manual entitled *Revolutionary War, Guerrillas and Communist Ideology* even rendered participation in the democratic process itself as beyond the pale for alleged insurgents. It argued that guerrillas can 'resort to subverting the government by means of elections in which the insurgents cause the replacement of an unfriendly government official to one favourable to their cause … insurgent leaders can participate in political races as candidates for government posts'.[31] In effect, then, avenues of dissent and processes of democratic lobbying for reform were designated as inimical to the overall CI effort to such an extent that protests, petitions and even letter-writing to local newspapers were considered to be 'insurgent activity indicators' demonstrating that insurgents were influencing society 'toward revolution'.[32] US CI strategy was thus directly at odds with broad swathes of democratic activity.

Paramilitary units were to form the vanguard for both monitoring and intelligence-gathering on alleged enemy civilians and civil society organizations. In training paramilitary forces an early US CI field manual, entitled *US Army Counterinsurgency Forces*, explains that 'paramilitary units can support the national army in the conduct of counterinsurgency operations when the latter are being conducted in their own province or political subdivision', with assistance 'for organizing, equipping, and training paramilitary forces' being 'provided through the [US] Military Assistance Program, the US AID Mission (for civil police), or other elements of the Country Team'.[33] In a section entitled 'Secure Population Centers', the manual outlines how 'mobile reserves' that are 'generally made up of paramilitary units' can be used to 'move rapidly to the assistance' of villages under attack from insurgent forces. These paramilitaries were also to be involved in the establishment 'of an intelligence network in the community for the purpose of developing information about guerrillas in the area and to insure the prompt exposure of any undercover insurgent sympathizers in the community'. The manual goes on to list a series of measures that could be introduced to further control civilian populations. These include the suspension 'of civil rights to permit search of persons ... and arrest and confinement on suspicion', the 'establishment of a reporting system whereby absentee employees are immediately reported for investigation', the confiscation of 'property, real and personal, of those individuals adjudged guilty of collaboration', press 'censorship', and the forced 'relocation of entire hamlets or villages [or] suspected individuals and families to unfamiliar neighborhoods, away from relatives and friends who may be serving with the insurgents'.[34]

We see, then, a very clear development of US strategy that entrenched a militarized relationship between Latin American militaries and their own populations. As part of this reorientation, US military aid and training openly advocated the use of terrorism and violence as a legitimate part of the overall CI effort. When we marry these techniques of coercive statecraft with the inherent designation of progressive social forces such as labour unions, teachers' organizations and student protest as 'subversive', the end result is deadly. Communism became the principal referent for subversion, with communism allegedly manifested through *any* challenges to what were highly class-stratified societies throughout Latin America. Moreover, conservative pro-US militaries became the ultimate arbiter as to what constituted subversion. Thus, the 'refusal of peasants to pay rent, taxes, or loan payments', the 'appearance of questionable doctrine in the educational system' or even an 'increase of petitions demanding government redress of grievances'[35] became indicators of communist insurgency. The use of CI strategy and discourse was operationalized through its legitimating function for repressive military responses to reform that in turn served to defend the interests of Latin America's pro-US indigenous ruling classes and insulate political and economic structures favourable to the US imperial state. Crucially, then, counter-insurgency both served a coercive policing function *and* provided a discursive framework to defend and maintain pro-US capitalist socio-economic relations throughout Latin America, with devastating consequences for human rights. I now develop this argument more fully with an examination of the ways in which US CI policy and discourse were mapped on to Colombia during the Cold War.

Antecedents to US CI in Colombia: *la violencia*

Since the late 1840s the Conservative and Liberal parties have dominated Colombian politics.[36] The Conservative Party has historically aligned with and represented the interests of the large landholding oligarchy and the Catholic Church. The Liberal Party, on the other hand, has been more closely aligned with Colombia's commercial sector and tended to view the Catholic Church as a backward social institution that prevented economic modernization. Although for many years their policy programmes were largely indistinguishable, the rise of Jorge Gaitan, a left-wing Liberal Party member during the 1940s, managed to reorient the Liberal Party towards a more reformist and egalitarian agenda that sought modest land reforms and progressive labour laws.[37] Gaitan's populism was based on his appeal to the poor and dispossessed throughout Colombia; in the words of Jenny Pearce, he sought to make 'capitalism socially responsible, not to abolish it'.[38] Gaitan took over the leadership of the Liberal Party in 1947, and was almost certain to win elections scheduled for 1950. But Gaitan's increasingly populist appeal, combined with his overt rhetoric attacking the unequal distribution of national resources, made Colombia's ruling class, and especially the large landowners aligned with the Conservative Party, increasingly worried and hostile. Gaitan was subsequently assassinated in Bogotá (Colombia's capital city) in 1948. His assassination ended the democratic challenge to oligarchic rule in Colombia, and destroyed the hopes of the poor majority that he represented. His death also 'ruptured the breakwaters holding back years of discontent' and the immediate response to his assassination was a spontaneous popular uprising in Bogotá that destroyed established symbols of power and privilege.[39] The Colombian military put down the uprising but the violence spread to Colombia's rural areas and sparked a large-scale civil war within Colombia now known as *la violencia*. This civil war lasted for almost ten years and pitted rural Conservative and Liberal peasants against each other. It is estimated that up to 200,000 people died during this period, and the resolution of the violence was achieved through the formation in 1958 of a National Front rotational government between both the Liberal and Conservative parties.[40] This served to alternate power between the differently aligned sections of the Colombian Conservative and Liberal elite while strengthening the Colombian armed forces to suppress popular reforms and the remaining armed partisans in the rural areas.

In relation to the USA, the instability triggered by Gaitan's assassination and the emergence of armed Liberal and Conservative guerrillas in Colombia's rural areas was interpreted as dangerously threatening to US interests. The USA sought to stabilize the Colombian political system which threatened to disintegrate as a result of the instability caused by *la violencia*; in 1948–49 alone, for example, two Colombian governments collapsed.[41] The US Department of State recognized these dangers and declared the crisis in Colombia to be threatening 'because of strategic, political and economic considerations' with 'Colombia's radical departure from customary practises' a 'vital concern to the United States'.[42] The USA had substantial strategic interests in Colombia due to its proximity to the crucial sea lane of the Panama Canal. For example, Colonel Edward Lansdale, then US Assistant Secretary of Defense for Special Operations, argued for comprehensive engagement by the USA to protect its access to the Panama Canal: 'During the expected two years remaining in the Presidency of Lleras Camarago, there is a real opportunity for the U.S. to undertake assistance to Colombia to correct the situation of political insurrection which reportedly has caused a quarter-million deaths and displaced over a million and a half people since 1948 in this area neighboring a place so vital to our own national security as the Canal Zone.'[43] The USA also had significant economic interests in Colombia specifically and South America more generally. In 1959, for example, Colombia was one of the largest markets in South America for US direct foreign investment (FDI). In 1959, of the $399 million of US FDI in Colombia, the vast majority was in oil ($225 million), followed by manufacturing, public utilities and trade.[44]

The USA also feared both the internal and regional instability that could be triggered by the remaining armed bands in Colombia's southern regions. In particular the USA feared the potential threat that these armed bands posed to capitalism. A 1959 US memo outlined the rationale for the provision of US CI military aid to Colombia: 'it would be difficult to make the finding of present Communist danger in the Colombian guerrilla situation'; however, 'the continuance of unsettled conditions in Colombia contributes to Communist objectives' and threatens the 'establishment of a pro-US, free enterprise democracy'.[45] In response to the perceived crisis, the USA began to provide Colombia with increased military aid. This aid was designed both to insulate the National Front arrangement from popular pressures for reform by using the Colombian military to suppress the peasantry, and also to strengthen the Colombian military in its increasingly counter-guerrilla strategy directed against the remnants of armed peasant groups left over from the years of la violencia. Total US military aid for Latin America between 1950 and 1957 was $156 million with Colombia receiving $18.3 million; over 11 per cent of the total for Latin America as a whole.[46]

In 1958, the US ambassador to Colombia, John Cabot, explained that if 'we wish Colombia to undertake further military programs ... in our interest [then] we must also pay for them', with US aid and training increasing Colombia's 'friendliness for the United States'.[47] However, it was not until the late 1950s and early 1960s that the USA explicitly reoriented the Colombian military away from an externally-orientated hemispheric defence posture to an internal security arrangement to deal with the remaining armed guerrillas spread throughout Colombia's rural areas. Although the armed groups were not seen as linked to the Soviet Union's alleged expansionist tendencies, the very presence of the groups and their challenge to the authority of the Colombian state were interpreted as dangerous to US interests. These 'unsettled conditions' led the USA to offer 'to send to Colombia a team of experts on guerrilla warfare problems, to survey the situation and make recommendations to President Lleras with respect to an overall program to eliminate the problem'.[48] A US Special Survey Team that was comprised of US CI experts who had previously served in developing countries including the Philippines and parts of Asia and Latin America arrived in Colombia in October 1959.[49] The team recommended a series of actions that both the USA and Colombia should undertake in setting up an effective CI orientation for the Colombian military. These actions began the process of reorienting the Colombian military for an internal security role, and inculcating the CI discourse. For Colombia the survey team recommended the establishment of dedicated CI brigades, the setting up of an effective military intelligence network, improved training methods and the rehabilitation of the national police into a formalized CI structure. The US role was primarily related to training and the provision of military aid along with an overall advisory role.[50]

The initial survey team's findings were augmented in 1962 by a follow-up survey conducted by a US Army Special Warfare team led by General William Yarborough. Yarborough's principal objective was to 'make recommendations for [the] utilization of a US counterinsurgency MTT [Mobile Training Team]'. These MTTs consisted of US Special Forces trainers who would travel to Colombia to train Colombian military personnel in CI. Yarborough's recommendations give an insight into the early formulation of US policy in Colombia, and the US role in the development of clandestine paramilitary forces and their use by the Colombian state. Specifically, Yarborough stated:

> It is the considered opinion of the survey team that a concerted country team effort should be made now to select civilian and military personnel for clandestine training in resistance operations in case they are needed later. This should be done with a view toward development of a civil and military structure for exploitation in the event that the Colombian internal security system deteriorates further. This structure should be used to pressure toward reforms known to be needed, perform counter-agent and counter-propaganda functions and as necessary execute paramilitary, sabotage and/or terrorist activities against known communist proponents. It should be backed by the United States … The apparatus should be charged with clandestine execution of plans developed by the United States Government toward defined objectives in the political, economic and military fields. This would permit passing to the offensive in all fields of endeavor rather than depending on the Colombians to find their own solution.[51]

Yarborough's recommendations clearly illustrate the designation of particular social identities within the CI discourse as legitimate targets for attack and his recommendations are rather candid about the methods to be used by US-backed CI forces. Also interesting is the insight that his recommendations give into the attribution of responsibility for state terror in Colombia in so far as he calls for an offensive US strategy in place of Colombian solutions to their own perceived problems ('This would permit passing to the offensive in all fields of endeavor rather than depending on the Colombians to find their own solution'). The intelligence assessment goes on to provide clear indications of the development of the CI discourse within Colombian military doctrine and its institutional links to US training and aid. One of the designated objectives of the US CI intelligence mission in Colombia was the introduction of 'anti-communist indoctrination [for all Colombian] services schools, [the] Military Academy and [the] War College' and the reorientation of the Colombian military to develop 'an appreciation of the western democratic system and culture' that would serve to inculcate 'anti-communist indoctrination' for US-trained forces. The assessment was also quite frank as to the methods to be used to imbue senior Colombian military officials with the CI discourse:

> [F]rom the beginning it was considered that in order to adequately influence and capture the minds of present and future [Colombian] Armed Forces leaders, with the objective of orientating them to western democratic concepts and precepts, much more was required than just obvious simple publications expounding on the virtues of western democracy and the evils of communism. It was deemed necessary to use the gentle indirect approach, which would expand their mental horizons and imbue them with the spirit and great universal thoughts of great thinkers and writers of all ages, who believed in the virtue of a free society in all fields of endeavour ... Coupled with the above an approximate total of 225,000 copies of direct anti-communist type of literature and security was distributed to the Armed Forces units and personnel as well as civilians during various civic action 'Jornadas' of many military units ... Another media [sic] was the utilization of numerous movies depicting the tragedy, misery and inhumanness of communism. These were distributed for showing in every Army headquarters and unit down to and including company level.[52]

This makes clear the conscious strategy of the USA to inculcate the CI discourse within the Colombian military, and foster the perception of insurgency as externally sponsored. Ultimately, Yarborough's recommendations went on to form the core of the USA's reorganization of Colombian military forces, whose new counter-insurgency strategy debuted with the implementation of 'Plan Lazo' between 1962 and 1965.

US policy, Plan Lazo and paramilitarism

Plan Lazo was designed to destroy the various armed groups in Colombia's rural areas left over from the years of la violencia and was principally targeted at the peasant agriculturalists found in Colombia's south. These areas were largely populated by peasants who had either fled the violence of the civil war or were dispossessed through land clearances. According to Jenny Pearce, these peasant communities 'farmed the land and organized their own defense' and had 'no broader political project'.[53] However, the independence of these areas from Colombian state control combined with the continued existence of armed groups left over from the years of *la violencia* were interpreted as dangerous to US interests, largely because of the perceived potential for these areas to become hotbeds of opposition to the government. A US State Department memorandum argued that 'Our National Policy Paper on Colombia ... sets forth one of our principal objectives as the elimination of the potential for subversive insurgency inherent in the continued existence of active bandit groups, guerilla bands, and communist dominated "enclaves"' in Colombia's south.[54] In dealing with these perceived problems Colombian President Guillermo León Valencia (1962–66) gave the Colombian military a free hand in its CI campaign by declaring a 'state of siege' whereby the government transferred judicial and political powers to the military with little to no civilian oversight of its operations. Human Rights Watch has documented how this 'state of siege' has been the norm for most of Colombia's post-war history. Decrees passed while under the siege have later been incorporated into Colombian law. For example, Decree 3398, passed in 1965 as part of Plan Lazo, essentially 'laid the legal foundation for the active involvement of civilians in the war from 1965 until 1989' and was converted into Colombian law in 1968. This new law (Law 48) 'authorized the executive to create civil patrols by decree and for the Defense Ministry to provide them with "weapons restricted to the exclusive use of the armed forces"'. Law 48 was then 'frequently cited ... as the legal foundation for their support for all paramilitaries'.[55] The Colombian military followed Yarborough's recommendations in selecting and training key civilians to work alongside the Colombian military in its CI campaign, and paramilitary 'civil defense' forces were set up by and incorporated within Colombian military networks.

One of the earliest uses of paramilitary forces under the rubric of CI warfare was the development of a CI intelligence infrastructure within Plan Lazo that used civilian paramilitary forces to gather intelligence for the overall CI effort and was in turn linked to 'official' Colombian CI forces. Civilian irregulars were central in manning the intelligence network and the system was designed to 'link together the battalions in I, III, VI, and VIII Brigade areas to the civilian populace and authorities, to local and national police and to the air force'.[56] This intelligence network was supplied and trained by the USA. A US intelligence assessment of the communications network outlines its use within Plan Lazo:

To augment the Intelligence/Counterinsurgency capability, 3 GIL's (Intelligence Hunter/Killer Teams) were trained for use in the Marquetalia and Santander areas, 3 more are being trained for operations in the VI Brigade area, namely the communist influenced areas as El Pato, Gualuro, and Marquetalia. These teams of 25 officers, NCOs and civilians, are hard hitting, heavily armed, entities composed of selected veterans. They operate as a unit or divided into three segments, and use any disguise or stratagem to obtain their objective; they are trained to remain in the field for weeks and even months if required. They are capable not only of fighting, but of penetrating inimical groups and working with informants.[57]

Plan Lazo's major offensive against the peasants within the south concentrated on the Marquetalia region. 'Operation Marquetalia' involved a third of the Colombian military (16,000 US-supplied Colombian troops) that encircled the region. The strategy combined heavy artillery bombardments, the use of the Colombian air force and the highly mobile light infantry 'Hunter/Killer' paramilitary units to penetrate and destroy the peasant enclaves. Ostensibly, Plan Lazo and its largest strategic deployment in Marquetalia was a success in so far as the geographical areas of the independent republics were placed under Colombian military control. However, the majority of the armed peasantry that made up the independent republics escaped and formed a collective self-defence organization called the 'bloc of the South' in 1964. At a later conference in 1966, the Revolutionary Armed Forces of Colombia (FARC) were formed from this embryonic structure, and took their inspiration from the Cuban revolution.[58] The FARC essentially acted as a defensive organization with deep roots among the peasant colonizers, and acted to protect their interests from large cattle ranchers aligned with the Colombian military. They also provided basic social services in the absence of the Colombian state. As such, the FARC enjoyed a great deal of support among the disenfranchised peasant population and increased their power over the years.[59] In addition to the FARC, a much smaller guerrilla organization called the People's National Liberation Army (ELN), which was more closely aligned with Colombia's left-wing urban intelligentsia, emerged from the 1966 conference.

With the continued existence of an increasingly coordinated guerrilla movement in Colombia linked to peasant and working communities combined with the National Front, which continued to retard Colombia's political system, the USA sustained its CI military aid for a protracted CI war and the suppression of civil unrest. By 1967, for example, total

US military aid to Colombia had reached $160 million,[60] the largest amount for any Latin American nation prior to the El Salvadoran crisis during the 1980s. US CI support for Colombia continued uninterrupted throughout the Cold War, and it was not until the early 1980s that the Colombian state moved in any significant way from the policy of outright CI warfare embodied by Plan Lazo. In 1984, President Belisario Betancur negotiated a ceasefire with the FARC and a much smaller guerrilla movement called M19, and also began to open up the space for democratic alternatives to Liberal and Conservative domination of Colombia's political process. This was unprecedented in Colombian history and represented a major change from the previous all-out militarized focus of joint US–Colombian strategy.

The Colombian peace process and the democratic opening

While Colombia had enjoyed a relatively stable economy through the 1960s and 1970s, the vast majority of Colombians remained locked out of economic growth. This was true throughout the 1980s. Colombia's National Administrative Bureau of Statistics showed that, in 1986, 40 per cent of Colombians lived in poverty and 18 per cent in absolute poverty (defined as being unable to meet basic nutritional needs). At the same time the 'top three percent of Colombia's landed elite own[ed] 71.3 percent of arable land, while fifty-seven percent of the poorest farmers subsist on 2.8 percent'.[61] This poverty, which was most acute among rural inhabitants, led to a large rural-to-urban migration. In 1951, 61 per cent of Colombians lived in rural areas, whereas in 1983 only 26 per cent did.[62] These migrants often lived within shanty towns on the outskirts of Colombia's urban conurbations. These poor conditions and the rise of an urban underclass led to an upsurge in urban protests, strikes and support for Colombia's guerrilla movements. Although the National Front arrangement was formally dismantled in 1974, the clientilism of Liberal and Conservative Party politics continued to dominate Colombian politics during the 1980s, as did the interests that both of the parties served.

With the continued growth of the guerrilla movements, the more visible presence of poverty within Colombia's urban conurbations, and the failure of the Colombian military to eradicate the guerrillas, President Betancur began a peace process in 1982. This was the first of its kind within Colombia and commenced with an amnesty for guerrilla fighters signed by Betancur in 1982.[63] The amnesty freed a number of gaoled guerrilla fighters and also provided incentives (such as financial credits, land and housing) for the guerrillas to re-enter civilian life. Betancur also set up a Peace Commission to advise him on the peace process, and to meet and negotiate with guerrilla representatives. In return, a number of Colombia's guerrilla organizations agreed to a ceasefire in 1984. The peace process also attempted to open up Colombia's traditionally bipartisan political system to more reform-minded parties. The FARC 'was particularly interested in the government's promotion of reforms that would facilitate meaningful participation in Colombia's political life'.[64] As a result, the FARC established the Patriotic Union (UP) as a broad political movement to represent the left in Colombian politics and to articulate peasant and working-class interests within a democratic framework. According to sociologist Ricardo Vargas Meza: '[b]y incorporating some of the FARC's socio-economic demands and extending the cease-fire, the accords opened the possibility of a political resolution to the conflict. Betancur's position was a radical departure from that of his predecessors, for he recognized that guerrilla violence was the product of real social conditions and he understood the relationship between those conditions and the demands of the insurgents.'[65] The UP's political programme called for political reforms to end the Conservative and Liberal domination of Colombian politics, the popular election of local mayors, rural land reforms and the nationalization of foreign businesses, Colombian banks and transportation.[66]

Despite the ongoing peace process and the ceasefire, the Colombian military and paramilitaries, backed by the USA, stepped up their CI offensives against the guerrilla groups and Colombian civilians. In particular, the military retained control of large parts of Colombia's rural areas. Human Rights Watch reported that most of the Colombian military's 'security measures' were designed to control the 'local residents' in militarized areas. The Colombian military also continued to attack the guerrillas and assassinate amnestied former fighters.[67] Americas Watch reported that, in the first year of peace negotiations, 'Large parts of the country are exclusively governed by the armed forces. To all intents and purposes, the armed forces are answerable only to themselves. Where the armed forces are the only government, their rule is harsh. It is marked by torture and massacres.'[68]

A later report confirmed that many 'of the corpses that are found after disappearances bear distinctive marks of torture ... probably practiced during interrogation'.[69] Paramilitary activity also continued unabated as the peace process went on with 266 murders carried out in 1982, 433 in 1983 and 310 in 1984. A number of new paramilitary groups also emerged during the peace process (with names such as the Black Hand and National-Socialist Worker–Student Movement). Alongside the rise of these new paramilitary groups, throughout the 1980s a 'reverse land reform' occurred whereby lands formerly inhabited by peasant agriculturalists in Colombia's rural areas were taken over by drug warlords who, in turn, used the land to cultivate coca and set up paramilitary networks to defend their interests. The largest drug-funded paramilitary group was called Death to Kidnappers (Muerte a Secuestradores or MAS) and was set up in 1981 by the Medellin drug cartel to target the insurgents and their alleged civilian sympathizers. It also provided the prototype for the emergence of a new kind of paramilitary phenomenon explicitly tied to the drugs trade and the defence of the interests of the increasingly powerful coca-funded 'narcobourgeois'.[70] (In 1982 MAS killed ninety-six people, issued a number of death threats and was responsible for forty-six counts of torture.)[71] Americas Watch reported that these drug-financed paramilitary groups 'perform a variety of functions: they can act as "civil defense groups" to resist guerrilla pressures; they provide security for coca plantations, emerald mines and cattle ranches ... [and also] perform complicated kidnappings and murders ... as well as to commit mass killings'. The groups 'are assisted by large landowners' who, along with 'managers for other business concerns (such as mines and fruit plantations), finger targets for the killings', while local and 'regional military chiefs provide intelligence on the identity and whereabouts of some targets, and contribute the crucial factor of impunity for the perpetrators'.[72] Common to these paramilitary organizations were their targets that included 'members of the rural community, peasant or labor organizations or persons suspected of sympathizing with or aiding the guerrillas', as well as their links to the Colombian military and powerful sectors of Colombian society.[73] For example, MAS was supported by and made up of Colombian military operatives. In 1983 the Colombia Procurator General released a report 'naming fifty-nine active-duty military men among the 163 members of MAS he had been able to identify'.[74] A large number of these military men had been trained in the SOA, with Colombian General, Ramón Emilia Gil Bermúdez, invited back to the SOA as a guest speaker in 1988, five years after his involvement in MAS had been exposed.[75]

The UP was particularly hard hit by Colombian military and paramilitary forces during the peace process and beyond. Despite the fact that it was formed only in 1985, coupled with its modest resources and the repression its activists had suffered at the hands of the paramilitaries, the UP had enjoyed some success in the 1986 national elections and managed to secure 5 per cent of the votes. It had also had a number of mayors, council officers, congress people and senators elected.[76] Although attacks on UP members had occurred prior to the election, the modest success of the UP triggered a wave of repression by Colombian military and paramilitary forces. By 1990, two of its presidential candidates had been assassinated while at least 846 party members had been killed.[77] By the mid-1990s over 3,000 UP activists had been murdered by Colombian paramilitary forces. Javier Giraldo has documented that since the UP's foundation, a UP member has been assassinated every fifty-three hours, and in the run-up to post-1986 elections the assassinations have increased to one every twenty-six hours.[78] In the same year that the UP was established, the United Confederation of Workers (CUT) was formed. It consisted of a majority of Colombia's trade unions and was designed to represent democratically workers' interests in negotiations with both the Colombian state and employers. Like the UP, the CUT suffered severe repression with 230 members murdered in its first year alone, most of whom had been found to have been 'brutally tortured' (according to the North American NGO, the Washington Office on Latin America).[79] Similarly, the vast majority of those disappeared in Colombia – abducted and later found murdered – continued to be trade unionists, human rights workers and grassroots organizers. In 1989, a UN Working Group concluded that in the majority of cases circumstantial evidence 'strongly suggests or precise information clearly demonstrates involvement of units of the armed forces or security services in enforced or involuntary disappearances'.[80] This repression, particularly against the UP, has served to perpetuate the violence in Colombia and insulate Colombia's political system from reformist pressures.

Particularly telling was US support for the Colombian military throughout the peace process. The USA consistently failed to condemn human rights abuses committed by Colombian military personnel in its annual human rights reports produced by the State Department.[81] The most significant aspect of US policy was the continued flow of arms and CI training for the Colombian military throughout the peace process. In 1984 alone (the year of the official 'ceasefire'), the USA sent over $50 million in arms to Colombia's security forces. With the symbiotic relationship between the Colombian military and paramilitary forces, US military aid was by extension also ending up with the paramilitary groups; moreover, the School of the Americas trained 4,844 Colombian personnel in CI between 1984 and 1990.[82] US military aid and training for CI thus served both to legitimize the repression of the Colombian military and effectively to undermine the peace negotiations. What can we conclude from this account?

This chapter has argued that US CI strategy became the principal form of US coercive statecraft throughout Latin America during the Cold War. Officially, US CI strategy was justified by reference to the bipolar confrontation. As illustrated above, the USA officially viewed insurgency as either providing conditions for possible communist expansion or as an actual manifestation of Soviet expansionism: 'Recent history has been characterized by the frequent occurrences of insurgencies which have usually taken place in developing and/or emerging nations ... Frequently, such insurgencies have been Communist inspired or have become subversive in nature ... In recent years the Communists have instigated or supported insurgencies in many parts of the world as a means of expanding their sphere of influence and/or control.'[83] However, this chapter has shown that within the CI discourse promulgated by US CI strategists, communist insurgency was defined so broadly as to encompass practically any form of dissent. Through its designation and construction of any type of reformism or progressive political activity as inherently subversive, coupled with the open advocacy of state terrorism, US CI strategy served to legitimate widespread repression while protecting and preserving social orders deemed favourable to US interests. The legacy of this discourse is clear: the vast majority of the victims of CI warfare have been non-combatants.[84]

Colombia's political system has long been designed to function in the interests of its minority elite. The political instability generated by the assassination of Gaitan and the resolution of this crisis through the formation of the National Front arrangement served further to entrench the power of Colombia's elites. The FARC, along with other guerrilla organizations, grew out of rural inequality, state violence and the failure of Colombia's political system to accommodate any moves democratically to redress Colombia's vastly unequal distribution of national resources. Furthermore, US CI strategy was explicitly set up to defend the National Front arrangement through the pacification of both the armed insurgents and popular pressures for socio-economic reform. The peace process that began in the early 1980s attempted to restructure Colombia's relationship to the guerrilla groups and open up Colombia's democratic system. The USA remained hostile to the negotiations throughout the peace process and most tellingly US military aid and training for the Colombian military continued unabated while new paramilitary groups were being formed by the Colombian military to exterminate UP members and civilians deemed inimical. In sum, US CI strategy has sought to insulate the Colombian state from popular pressures for reform. The principal mechanism for this strategy has been the use of widespread and pervasive state terrorism, justified under the rubric of Cold War anti-communism.

Despite the end of the Cold War, US military aid has not only continued but towards the end of the 1990s it radically increased and made Colombia the third largest recipient of US military aid in the world. However, accompanying this increasing military aid has been a change in the discourses justifying this aid. These discourses have switched from an official justification of anti-communism to anti-narcotics and, post-September 11, a new 'war on terror'.

Notes

1 Schoultz, *National Security and United States Policy Towards Latin America*; see also LeoGrande, *Our Own Backyard*.

2 On the development of US counter-insurgency and its use more generally see D. Michael Shafer, *Deadly Paradigms. The Failure of US Counterinsurgency Policy* (Princeton, NJ: Princeton University Press, 1988).

3 Rostow, *The Stages of Economic Growth*.

4 David Bell, *The Role of AID in Development and Internal Defense* (Boston, MA: John F. Kennedy Library, 1964).

5 Schmitz, *Thank God They're on Our Side*.

6 US Congress, *The Foreign Assistance Act*, 1961, Chapter 22, Title 32, Section 501. <http://projects.sipri.se/expcon/natexpcon/USA/USC2301.htm>

7 Klare and Kornbluh (eds), *Low Intensity Warfare*.

8 Nelson-Pallmeyer, *School of Assassins*.

9 Patterson quoted in McClintock, *The American Connection*, pp. 8–9.

10 Gearoid O Tuathail and John Agnew, 'Geopolitics and Discourse: Practical Geopolitical Reasoning in American Foreign Policy', *Political Geography*, 11, 1992, pp. 192–3.

11 For more on the role of power and knowledge within discourses and their link to institutions see Michel Foucault, *Discipline and Punish: The Birth of the Prison* (New York: Vintage, 1977).

12 US Department of the Army, *US Army Counterinsurgency Forces*, FM31-22, 1963, p. 85.

13 US Army Special Warfare School, *Concepts for US Army Counterinsurgency Activities* (Fort Bragg, 1962), p. II-K-8. <http://www.adtdl.army.mil/rtddltextv.html>

14 US Department of the Army, *Counter-Insurgency Operations*, 1 December 1960, quoted in McClintock, *Instruments of Statecraft*, pp. 105–7. McClintock's book is an excellent study of the doctrinal evolution of CI from its early incorporation of Nazi methods of counter-partisan warfare applied in Eastern Europe during the Second World War up to its application in Central America during the 1980s.

15 US Department of the Army, *Psychological Operations*, FM33-5, 1962, pp. 122, 125, 115–16.

16 Department of Defense, US Army School of the Americas, *Manejo de Fuente*, pp. 65, 66, 26; translated by the *National Security Archive* and accessed at

<http://www.gwu.edu/~nsarchiv/nsa/archive/news/dodmans.htm> See also Latin American Working Group, *Declassified Army and CIA Manuals*, February 1997. <http://www.lawg.org/pages/new%20pages/Misc/Publications-manuals.htm>

17 See the *Federation of Associations for Relatives of the Detained-Disappeared* website at <http://www.desaparecidos.org/fedefam/eng.html> for more on Enforced Disappearances. For background on some of the issues see Jeanette Bautista, *Enforced Disappearances and Impunity in Latin America*, European Union Committee on Foreign Affairs, Security and Defence Policy: Subcommittee on Human Rights, October 1996. <http://www.europarl.eu.int/hearings/impunity/latinam2_en.htm>

18 FEDEFAM, *Fighting Against Forced Disappearances in Latin America*, n.d. <http://www.desaparecidos.org/fedefam/eng.html>

19 On the use of torture by US-backed Latin American states see Brown (ed.), *With Friends Like These*.

20 Central Intelligence Agency, *Human Resource Exploitation Training Manual*, 1983. <http://www.gwu.edu/~nsarchiv/NSAEBB/NSAEBB27/> For background see Dana Priest, *Washington Post*, 21 September 1996.

21 Central Intelligence Agency, *KUBARK Counterintelligence Interrogation Manual*, 1963. <http://www.kimsoft.com/2000/kub_iii.htm> For background see Tom Blanton, *The CIA in Latin America*, National Security Archive, 14 March 2000. <http://www.gwu.edu/~nsarchiv/NSAEBB/NSAEBB27/index.html>

22 *Baltimore Sun*, 27 January 1997. <http://eagle.westnet.gr/~cgian/ciatortu.htm>

23 See for example Bruce Campbell and Arthur Brenner (eds), *Death Squads in Global Perspective: Murder with Deniability* (New York: St Martin's Press, 2000); Sluka (ed.), *Death Squad*.

24 McClintock, *Instruments of Statecraft*.

25 Joint Chiefs of Staff, 'Combined GVN-US Efforts to Intensify Pacification Efforts in Critical Provinces', 19 June 1964, quoted in George (ed.), *Western State Terrorism*, p. 139.

26 US Department of the Army, *US Army Handbook of Counterinsurgency Guidelines for Area Commanders. An Analysis of Criteria*, no. 550-100, 1966, p. 225. Although 'genocide' was not 'an alternative' to 'selective counter-terror', genocide was indeed practised by the Guatemalan military during the early 1980s.

27 US Department of the Army, *US Army Counterinsurgency Forces*, FM31-22, 1963, p. 8.

28 The manual I refer to here is the US Army School of the Americas, *Inteligencia de Combate*, produced circa 1982. The Latin America Working Group (LAWG), a North American NGO, has translated parts of the manual from Spanish into English and made them available at their website: <http://www.lawg.org/manuals.htm> LAWG does not provide sources for the original English-language manuals used and instead relies on English translations of the Spanish manuals. However, the original English-language manual on which *Inteligencia de Combate* is based is US Department of the Army, *Stability Operations–Intelligence*, FM 30-21, 1970.

29 US Department of the Army, *Stability Operations – Intelligence*, FM 30-21, 1970, p. 4.

30 Quotations from ibid., pp. 43, 73–4, 77, 78, E1, E1–E7.

31 Quote from US Department of the Army, *Revolutionary War, Guerrillas and Communist Ideology*, 1989, p. 51, translated by Latin American Working Group, *Declassified Army and CIA Manuals*, February 1997. <http://www.lawg.org/pages/new%20pages/Misc/Publications-manuals.htm>

32 US Department of the Army, *Stability Operations – Intelligence: Appendix E*, FM 30-21, 1970, p. E1.

33 US Department of the Army, *US Army Counterinsurgency Forces*, FM31-22, 1963, p. 84.

34 Ibid., pp. 99,106–7.

35 US Department of the Army, *Stability Operations – Intelligence: Appendix E*, FM 30-21, 1970, pp. E1–E7.

36 Pearce, *Colombia*, p. 17; for a broader overview of Colombian history see Bushnell, *The Making of Modern Colombia*.

37 For a summary of Gaitan's rise through the Colombian Liberal Party and the events surrounding his assassination see Ruiz, *The Colombian Civil War*, pp. 38–60.

38 Pearce, *Colombia*, p. 45.

39 Washington Office on Latin America, *Colombia Besieged: Political Violence and State Responsibility* (Washington, DC: Washington Office on Latin America, 1989), p. 13.

40 For more on the years of *la violencia* see Gonalo Sánchez and Donny Meertens, *Bandits, Peasants, and Politics: The Case of 'La Violencia' in Colombia* (Austen: University of Texas Press, 2001).

41 Randall, *Colombia and the United States*, p. 196.

42 US Office of Intelligence Research, Untitled, 19 September 1950, quoted in ibid., p. 198.

43 US Department of State, *Preliminary Report, Colombia Survey Team, Colonel Lansdale*, 23 February 1960. <http://www.icdc.com/~paulwolf/colombia/lansdale23feb1960a.jpg>

44 Randall, *Colombia and the United States*, p. 241.

45 Memo from Mr Rubottom, *President Lleras' Appeal for Aid in Suppressing Colombian Guerrilla Warfare Activities*, 21 July 1959. <http://www.icdc.com/~paulwolf/colombia/rubottom21jul1959a.jpg>

46 Randall, *Colombia and the United States*, p. 202.

47 John Cabot quoted in ibid., p. 206.

48 Memo from Mr Rubottom, *President Lleras' Appeal for Aid in Suppressing Colombian Guerrilla Warfare Activities*, 21 July 1959. <http://www.icdc.com/~paulwolf/colombia/rubottom21jul1959.htm>

49 J. C. King, *Memorandum for John C. Hill: Team for Colombia*, 29 September 1959. <http://www.icdc.com/~paulwolf/colombia/surveyteam29sep1959.htm>

50 Author unknown, *Annex A – Colombia Survey Team Recommendations*

for US Action, circa 1965. <http://www.icdc.com/~paulwolf/colombia/g21965tabe.htm>

51 William Yarborough, Headquarters United States Army Special Warfare Center, *Subject: Visit to Colombia, South America, by a Team from Special Warfare Center, Fort Bragg. Supplement, Colombian Survey Report*, 26 February 1962. <http://www.icdc.com/~paulwolf/colombia/surveyteam26feb1962.htm>

52 Author unknown, *USARMIS Intelligence Effort in Colombia (1961–1965)*, circa 1965. <http://www.icdc.com/~paulwolf/colombia/g21965tabfb.jpg>

53 Pearce, *Colombia*, p. 64.

54 Robert W. Adams, *Memorandum to Mr Mann, Subject: Helicopters for Colombia*, 14 May 1964. <http://www.icdc.com/~paulwolf/colombia/lazoadams14may1964a.jpg>

55 Human Rights Watch/Americas Human Rights Watch Arms Project, *Colombia's Killer Networks: The Military–Paramilitary Partnership and the United States.* <http://www.hrw.org/reports/1996/killer2.htm> For more on Law 48 and its use in legitimating paramilitarism see Commission for the Study of Violence, 'Organized Violence', in Berquist et al. (eds), *Violence in Colombia*, pp. 261–72.

56 Rempe, 'Guerrillas, Bandits, and Independent Republics', pp. 304–27.

57 Author unknown, *USARMIS Intelligence Effort in Colombia (1961–1965)*, circa 1965. <http://www.icdc.com/~paulwolf/colombia/g21965tabf.htm>

58 Pearce, *Colombia*, p. 64; see also Richard Gott, *Guerrilla Movements in Latin America* (London: Nelson, 1970).

59 Pearce, *Colombia*, p. 167. See Alfredo Molano, 'Violence and Land Colonization', in Charles Berquist et al. (eds), *Violence in Colombia*, pp. 195–216 for an excellent overview of the growth of the FARC, its evolution from the independent republics and its links to peasant interests.

60 Pearce, *Colombia*, p. 63.

61 National Administrative Bureau of Statistics quoted in Washington Office on Latin America, *Colombia Besieged*, Washington, DC, pp. 8–9.

62 Americas Watch, *The Central-Americanization of Colombia? Human Rights and the Peace Process*, p. 11.

63 Ibid., p. 25.

64 Ibid., p. 38.

65 Ricardo Vargas Meza, 'The FARC, the War and the Crisis of State', *NACLA-Report on the Americas*, March/April 1998, p. 24.

66 Americas Watch, *The Central-Americanization of Colombia?*, p. 55.

67 Ibid., p. 113.

68 Americas Watch, *Human Rights in Two Colombia's: Functioning Democracy, Militarized Society* (New York: Americas Watch, 1982), p. 3.

69 Americas Watch, *The Killings in Colombia* (New York: Americas Watch, 1989), p. 79.

70 An early leader of MAS was Carlos Castano who would later go on to lead the United Self Defence Forces of Colombia (AUC), the paramilitary umbrella organization. See Ana Carrigan, 'The Career of Carlos Castano:

A Marriage of Drugs and Politics', *Crimes of War*, August 2001. <http://
www.crimesofwar.org/colombia-mag/career.html>

71 Americas Watch, *The Central-Americanization of Colombia?*, p. 104.

72 Americas Watch, *The Killings in Colombia*, pp. 56–7.

73 Americas Watch, *The Central-Americanization of Colombia?*, p. 115.

74 Ibid., p. 104.

75 Virtual Truth Commission, *Atrocities Committed in Colombia Involving
School of the Americas Graduates* < http://www.geocities.com/~virtualtruth/
colom_3.htm> For an extensive list of Colombian graduates of the SOA that
have gone on to commit violations of human rights see the website of the
human rights NGO Derechos Human Rights, *Notorious Colombian School of the
Americas Graduates*. <http://www.derechos.org/soa/colom-not.html>

76 Americas Watch, *The Killings in Colombia*, p. 44; for a good contextual
overview of the UP's history see Steven Dudley, *Walking Ghosts. Murder and
Guerrilla Politics in Colombia* (New York: Routledge, 2004).

77 Americas Watch, *Political Murder and Reform in Colombia* (Washington, DC:
Human Rights Watch, 1992), p. 4.

78 Javier Giraldo, p. 68.

79 Washington Office on Latin America, *Colombia Besieged*, p. 43.

80 United Nations Economic and Social Council, *Report of the Working Group
on Enforced or Involuntary Disappearances*, 6 February 1989, p. 33.

81 Washington Office on Latin America, *Colombia Besieged*, pp. 112–15.

82 Giraldo, *Colombia*, p. 12.

83 US Department of the Army, *Stability Operations – Intelligence*, FM 30-21,
1970, p. 4.

84 For more on this see Amnesty International's website: <http://
www.amnesty.org/>

5 | From communism to the war on terror

Since the end of the Cold War the USA has argued that its military objectives in Colombia have switched from Cold War anti-communist CI to a new strategy of counter-narcotics and counter-terrorism. On the face of it, this makes sense given the end of the Cold War. However, since the end of the Cold War the USA has continued to fund and support a pervasive strategy of CI in Colombia that has been reliant on the principal Colombian drug traffickers and terrorists. Alongside the continuity in this strategy has been a continuity in the targets, although there have been some changes in the means used. These targets continue to be both the armed insurgent movements and broad swathes of Colombian civil society that threaten US economic and strategic interests both in Colombia and in South America more broadly. What has in fact changed are the pretexts used to justify US policy, which have shifted from anti-communism to counter-drugs and counter-terrorism. Furthermore, and more crucially, these new pretexts serve to obscure the continuity of the USA's strategy of military funding and training for CI state terrorism that has made Colombia the world's third largest recipient of US military aid with over $2 billion given between 2000 and 2002 alone.[1]

While the USA had been providing some counter-narcotics assistance to Colombia since the mid-1970s, by the end of the Cold War the 'war on drugs' increasingly came to replace the 'war on communism' as the primary justification for continued US military aid to South American governments. A State Department counter-drug strategy paper argued in June 1989 that the Drug Enforcement Administration (DEA) in South America had to 'draw more equipment and doctrine from the military as the task at hand ceases to be the traditional law enforcement for which the agency was created'. The report added that the US goal 'should be a steady withdrawal of DEA' from a counter-drug role 'as military and economic assistance allows local [military] forces to take up these tasks'.[2] Then President George Bush Sr codified this new commitment when he argued that the 'logic is simple': in the new post-Cold War era the 'cheapest way to eradicate narcotics is to destroy them at their source' by wiping out 'crops wherever they are grown' and taking out the 'labs wherever they exist'.[3] He went on to argue that in the post-Cold War era the 'rules have changed. When requested, we will for the first time make available the appropriate resources of America's armed forces' for the new war on drugs.[4] As such, US military aid was increasingly sent through both general and counter-narcotics funding channels.

In September 1989 Bush announced the Andean Initiative, a five-year plan that sought to send $2.2 billion to the Andean countries of Bolivia, Peru and Colombia and which made these states the leading recipients of US military aid in Latin America.[5] For Colombia, a condition for receiving the aid was the restructuring of the economy to make it more open to the penetration of US capital. In 1990, in return for this 'economic opening' and the implementation of neo-liberal restructuring, the then Colombian President César Augusto Gaviria was rewarded with $65 million in US military aid and 100 US military advisers (mostly US special forces) to aid and assist Colombian security forces in their alleged new counter-narcotics role.[6] The neo-liberal reforms decreased tariffs on imported goods which in turn impacted negatively on Colombia's domestic economy and unemployment figures and contributed to a massive trade deficit of $4.2 billion eight years later.[7] Despite this, however, the US Congress passed Section 1004 of the National Defense Authorization Act in 1991 that reoriented US military aid and training towards the new war on drugs. Section 1004, for the first time, granted the US Department of Defense (DoD) the authority to transfer or fund 'transportation, reconnaissance, training, intelligence, and base support' for 'counternarcotic purposes'.[8] Section 1004 became one of the principal funding channels of US military aid to Colombia after the Cold War and remains one of the least transparent funding programmes run by the USA.[9]

From its inception the Andean Initiative radically expanded the role of the Colombian military, the US DoD, and the CIA in the new mission of counter-narcotics. Crucially, however, it also conflated insurgency movements with drug trafficking. For example, an Interagency Working Group Draft paper published just prior to the Andean Initiative outlined a number of different scenarios for US policy. The paper envisaged a comprehensive military and economic aid package and argued that 'counter-narcotics operations require the military to deal with insurgents' while 'better law enforcement and counterinsurgency efforts require better intelligence'. The counter-drug scenario outlined within the paper, and which subsequently most closely resembled that adopted by President Bush, was said to have 'the corollary benefit of helping democratic governments fight growing insurgent movements'.[10] National Security Directive 18, which outlined the programme finally adopted by the Bush administration, argued that the Andean Initiative 'will involve expanded assistance to indigenous police, military, and intelligence officials' and can be used to assist 'them to regain control of their countries from an insidious combination of insurgents and drug traffickers' with the 'common features' of counter-drug programmes in Peru, Bolivia and Colombia including an increased 'military assistance to neutralize guerrilla support for trafficking'.[11] Thus, from its inception the Andean Initiative linked insurgents and drug traffickers, and the eradication of 'narco-guerrillas' became the core justification for continued US military aid to Colombia. This represented a shift in the primary justification for US policy. While remaining consistently anti-insurgency, US national security interests were said to have shifted from the containment of insurgents allegedly linked to international communism to the containment of insurgents allegedly linked to international drug traffickers. In this way there remained continuity in the targets of US policy, but a discontinuity in its publicly stated rationale.

Alongside this justification, however, there existed a major discrepancy between the designation of the guerrillas as the principal drug traffickers to US markets and the views of the USA's lead agencies in the so-called war on drugs. Both the CIA and the DEA rejected the characterization of the Colombian insurgents as the primary drug traffickers. For example, a secret CIA report written in 1992 acknowledged that the FARC had become increasingly involved in drugs through their 'taxing' of the trade in areas under their geographical control and that in some cases the insurgents protected trafficking infrastructure to further fund their insurgency. The FARC have long taxed numerous businesses within their areas of control, and according to Nazih Richani have 'written codes of taxation' which have facilitated the accountability of the FARC to local businesses. The taxes raised tend to go towards sustaining the insurgency as well as providing local services such as schools and other social infrastructure. The FARC have also tended to act as arbiters between drug traffickers and peasant cultivators through the regulation of local markets through ensuring fair prices for peasant cultivators.[12] This has invariably led to tension between the FARC and traffickers, and this is confirmed by the CIA report. It states that relations between drug traffickers and the Colombian insurgents are 'characterized by both cooperation and friction'. The report also adds that although 'traffickers occasionally benefit from guerrilla protection, they resent the insurgents and have sometimes used force to resist their encroachment'. The report continues that 'we do not believe that the drug industry [in Colombia] would be substantially disrupted in the short term by attacks against guerrillas. Indeed, many traffickers would probably welcome, and even assist, increased operations against insurgents.'[13] A 1994 intelligence report produced by the DEA similarly argued that the interaction between insurgents and traffickers 'is characterized by both cooperation and conflict'. The report draws three major conclusions. First, any connections between the Colombian insurgents and drug trafficking organizations are merely ad hoc 'alliances of convenience'. Second, the independent involvement of the insurgents 'in Colombia's domestic drug production, transportation, and distribution is limited'. Third, and more crucially, however, the report concludes that the DEA 'has no evidence that [the insurgents] have been involved in the transportation, distribution, or marketing of illicit drugs in the United States or Europe'. It goes on to note that the 'DEA believes that the insurgents never will be major players in Colombia's drug trade'.[14] There was thus a significant discrepancy between the stated justifications for the continued funding of the Colombian military under the Andean Initiative and the views of the USA's own leading counter-drug organizations as to who exactly the principal drug trafficking organizations were. As the rest of this chapter shows, this linking of insurgent movements in Colombia with both drugs and international terrorism has remained consistent. Concomitantly, the key US counter-drug and international agencies within Colombia have remained consistent in arguing that Colombian insurgent movements are not the primary drug traffickers or indeed terrorists in Colombia. There thus exists a major discrepancy between the stated goals of US policy and the actual targets and effects.

From Bush to Clinton: the decertification of Colombia

Given the evidence of the CIA and DEA, it is unsurprising that Bush's Andean Initiative failed to make any significant changes to the amounts of drugs entering the USA. Indeed, in the first year of the Andean Initiative the price of heroin and cocaine entering the US dropped in value and increased in purity.[15] A 1994 RAND report confirmed this trend by showing that a supply-side 'war on drugs' was in fact the least effective way to control illegal narcotics entering the USA. The study found that providing treatment to cocaine users within the USA is ten times more effective at reducing drug abuse than drug interdiction schemes and twenty-three times more effective than the supply-side 'war on drugs'. The report continued that to achieve a 1 per cent reduction in US cocaine consumption, the United States could spend an additional $34 million on drug treatment programmes at home, or twenty times more, $783 million, on efforts to eradicate narcotics in source countries.[16] Despite these findings, under the presidency of Bill Clinton, US policy in Colombia continued to be overwhelmingly justified by counter-narcotics rhetoric with US aid remaining fairly consistent.[17]

Between 1996 and 1997, however, the policy of the Clinton administration is popularly perceived to have altered with US counter-narcotic assistance to Colombia delayed or cut off. This was in response to allegations that the then President of Colombia and leader of the Liberal Party, Ernesto Samper, whose presidency ran from 1994 until 1998, maintained links to drugs cartels.[18] The USA was also allegedly concerned about ongoing abuses of human rights by the Colombian military. These twin concerns led to the decertification of Colombia by the USA which, since the mid-1980s, has certified whether states in Latin America have been cooperating in its alleged war on drugs. Officially, this meant that Colombia would no longer receive military aid during the period of decertification.[19] Aside from the original Andean Initiative which shifted the stated rationale for the continuity of US security assistance to the Colombian military, the decertification of Colombia under Samper represents the most significant development in post-Cold War US policy towards Colombia prior to the major escalation of US aid in the late 1990s under Plan Colombia. Much has been made of this aid and training cut-off and it is frequently cited to support the argument that US policy in Colombia is overwhelmingly driven by counter-narcotics concerns and not by a CI strategy. The question is, if US policy is primarily characterized by CI, why did it eliminate military aid over concerns about the narcotics links between senior Colombian government officials and drug traffickers and the continued abuse of human rights by Colombian security forces?

Russell Crandall, for example, has argued that counter-narcotics and human rights concerns have always remained the 'overall priority' of post-Cold War US policy in Colombia.[20] Crandall has also cited the decertification of Colombia during the Samper years as evidence that US military aid was not connected to CI, and thus not implicated in human rights abuses committed by paramilitaries linked to the Colombian military. In critiquing my own work, Crandall has argued that 'it was during 1997 and 1998, when the US barely had contact with the Colombian military due to consecutive US decertification decisions, that the paramilitaries began their explosive increase in strength and numbers'.[21] The two programmes that were cut during the period of decertification were the USA's Foreign Military Financing (FMF) and the International Military Education and Training (IMET) programme. What is missing from this account, however, is the fact that while FMF and the State Department's IMET programme were frozen, other funding not only continued to flow but actually made up for the shortfall.[22] This continuity of 'security' assistance took two primary forms: the continued supply of arms and the continued training of Colombian security personnel for CI.

For example, in 1996 the USA supplied over $64 million in weapons combined with twelve Huey combat helicopters and twelve Blackhawk helicopters. The Blackhawks alone were sold to Colombia for $169 million.[23] These helicopters aided Colombian CI operations. In relation to the sale of the twelve Blackhawk helicopters, Barbara Larkin, Assistant Secretary of State for Legislative Affairs, argued that the Colombian army required the Blackhawks for a 'variety of missions' that included 'its own counter-narcotics operations' and 'counterinsurgency'. Although Larkin recognized that the Colombian army 'does not intend to use them solely for counter-narcotics purposes', this did not represent any problems, as the US State Department had not 'sought such assurances' for fear that the Colombian military might instead buy 'Russian, French or Canadian helicopters'.[24] In a background paper, the US State Department claimed that the sale of the Blackhawks to the Colombian army would 'allow the Army to conduct missions which have more of a guerrilla component'. In arguing for the sale of the helicopters to the army instead of the Colombian National Police (CNP), the State Department claimed: 'The CNP is, to a degree, less likely to find themselves in pitched fire-fights than the Army, which has primary responsibility for counterinsurgency missions.'[25] Another State Department background paper highlighted that the insurgents 'along with the traffickers' have 'been inflicting heavy casualties on government forces, both police and military', with the CNP taking '3000 casualties in this real war against these guerrillas and their drug trafficking allies'. The paper continued that the guerrillas have 'shot down 5 Huey helicopters and some eradication airplanes, as well'.[26]

A more plausible explanation for the decertification is that when the USA was presented with credible evidence that Samper had received funds from the Cali-based drug trafficking cartel, including the arrest and confession of Samper's presidential campaign manager, the USA faced a crisis of legitimacy in so far as it could not be seen to be dealing with a Colombian president so publicly linked to drug traffickers. The public decertification and the alleged military aid cut-off served to plug this legitimacy gap while shifting military funding to different channels, such as the State Department's International Narcotics Control (INC) programme. This is also clearly illustrated by the continuity of

US military training that was again allegedly frozen during the period of decertification. The Joint Command Exchange Training (JCET) programme is a US DoD-run programme that, in the words of Defense Department spokesman Kenneth Bacon, 'involves sending small teams of special forces people out to work with the militaries of other countries'.[27] According to the military officers involved in the JCET programme, civilian and State Department oversight of the programme was 'minimal, to nonexistent', with US Special Forces advisers training 'hundreds of Colombian troops in "shoot and maneuver" techniques, counter terrorism and intelligence gathering' during the period of decertification and the alleged security assistance cut-off.[28] Training under the JCET programme was said to be for counter-narcotics, but a senior US officer in Colombia explained that the US 'can call anything counter-drugs. If you are going to train to take out a target, it doesn't make much difference if you call it a drug lab or a guerrilla camp. There's not much difference between counter-drug and counterinsurgency.' He went on to explain, however, that the 'insurgency' word is no longer used, as 'it is politically too sensitive'.[29] More ominously, the JCET training conducted in Colombia was legally free of any restraints in relation to human rights. According to the *Washington Post*, US officers involved in the JCET missions in Colombia did not evaluate the Colombian military units being trained for potential human rights violations as this might 'interfere with the unit's ability to work together'.[30] US military training thus continued during the alleged period of decertification, with the line between what constitutes counter-narcotics and CI training for all intents and purposes non-existent. This was confirmed when I interviewed Stan Goff, a former US Special Forces trainer in Colombia:

> You were told, and the American public was being told, if they were told anything at all, that this was counter-narcotics training. The training I conducted was anything but that. It was pretty much updated Vietnam-style counter-insurgency doctrine. We were advised that this is what we would do, and we were further advised to *refer* to it as counter-narcotics training, should anyone ask. It was extremely clear to us that the counter-narcotics thing was an official cover story. The only thing we talked with the actual leaders of the training units about was the guerrillas.

When asked, 'Can counter-drug training be used for counter-insurgency, and what, if any, are the main differences?', Goff replied:

> The more instructive question might be, can counter-insurgency training be used for counter-drug training? The answer is, it depends. Certainly

there are some generic skills, shooting, navigating overland, planning and coordination, that apply to any kind of operation that has a quasi-military character. But not only did we not train counter-drug specific tasks, we weren't qualified to do so. This is the domain of police agencies. What official spokespersons will say, of course, is that the guerrillas *are* the narcotics traffickers. Therefore, the counter-insurgency doctrine is necessary to get to these 'narco-guerrillas'.[31]

It is clear, then, that the period of decertification did not represent a break or discontinuity in US policy towards Colombia, and in fact US military aid actually increased in relation to earlier years. The USA's General Accounting Office (GAO) stated as much when it admitted that the International Narcotics Control (INC) funding had 'more than doubled in 1997, in part to make up for shortfalls caused by the cut-off of FMF' during the period of decertification.[32]

As outlined above, during the period of decertification the insurgents became increasingly more confident, which in turn worried US planners. During the decertification period massive peasant mobilizations took place against Samper's government, while the Colombian army suffered a series of defeats by the guerrillas, which according to the National Security Archive were 'the most devastating actions taken by guerrilla groups in years'.[33] A senior US administration official observed that the Colombian government 'is in trouble' with 50 per cent of Colombian national territory no longer 'under government control'.[34] US military analysts had compiled reports on the growing strength of the FARC and 'counted 80 instances in which the FARC massed at least 300 men to attack army contingents and defeated the government troops every time'.[35] This led to the resumption of full US aid in September 1997, and early in 1998 the USA began officially to widen the scope of its aid to the Colombian military to encompass overt CI activities. According to the *Washington Post*, however, the aid was to be limited to a specific geographical area called 'the box' which covered 'roughly the southern half of the country' where the alleged 'alliance between the guerrillas and the drug traffickers is clearest'.[36] Thus, the Colombian military could now 'officially' use US-supplied arms and training for CI purposes in the areas where the insurgents were strongest. This provision, however, was amended in 2000, and according to the US Embassy in Colombia 'the box' was widened to encompass the 'entire national territory of the Republic of Colombia, including its territorial waters recognized by the International Law (sic), and its airspace'.[37] In short, all the conditions attached to US military aid were now officially loosened. Barry McCaffrey, then head of the US Office of National Drug Control Policy, argued that this widening of the official purpose of US military aid would serve to stem 'the ever expanding nexus between guerrilla movements ... and international drug trafficking organizations' that are an 'unprecedented threat to the rule of law, democratic institutions, and the very fabric of [Colombian] society'.[38] Under the presidency of Bill Clinton, US military aid to Colombia would reach unprecedented proportions.

Clinton's legacy: 'Plan Colombia'

Andres Pastrana was elected President of Colombia in 1999. Pastrana's election ended the twelve-year reign of the Liberal Party in Colombia, with Pastrana gaining 51 per cent of the vote.[39] According to the *New York Times*, after ten years of intensified neo-liberal reforms, Colombia was experiencing the 'worst recession in decades, a growing debt burden and an unemployment rate that has reached nearly 20 percent', which in turn added to the perception of Colombia as a country increasingly gripped by crisis.[40] However, this did not stop Pastrana advocating the intensification of neo-liberal reforms and the increased openness of Colombia's economy to the penetration of US transnational corporations. Pastrana also faced a crisis in so far as the FARC were becoming increasingly powerful in Colombia's southern regions where they had tended to concentrate their forces. This was recognized by US planners. Rand Beers, Assistant Secretary of State for International Narcotics and Law Enforcement Affairs, argued that, under Pastrana, 'Colombia stands at a critical crossroads' with 'considerable dangers for US interests, but also significant opportunities. The policy choices we make in the next several months and the assistance we provide could have a significant impact on Colombia's future, helping to determine whether it continues its long, slow descent toward chaos or begins to recover.'[41] The instability in Colombia was also linked to wider regional security and US interests. Madeleine Albright, then US Secretary of State, argued: 'Colombia's problems extend beyond its borders and have implications for regional security and stability.'[42] The policy choice eventually adopted by the Clinton administration was a massively expanded military aid programme called 'Plan Colombia'.

Pastrana originally proposed Plan Colombia as a $7.5 billion aid package designed to address the country's interwoven problems of extensive narco-trafficking, civil war and economic underdevelopment. The Plan's publicly explicit goals were the intensification of neo-liberal privatization, a negotiated peace process with the rebels and the eradication of narco-trafficking. A Colombian Foreign Ministry official argued that Colombia is 'working toward a much larger engagement with the United States, involving combating narcotics, strengthening our battlefield capabilities and economic issues ... It is a much broader engagement than just the narcotics issue because all our problems are linked.'[43] Four billion dollars was supposed to come from Colombia itself, mainly through the privatization of publicly owned utilities.[44] Pastrana called upon other countries and international lending organizations to supply the rest, with Albright stating that the 'United States has been working with the International Monetary Fund, the World Bank and other partners to insure that needed assistance is available' for Colombia.[45] Eventually, only a few European nations committed to the Plan with Spain committing the largest amount ($100 million). Most European countries held back primarily because of the militarized focus of US aid, which allocated $1.3 billion to the Plan, primarily in the form of military aid.[46] This money significantly changed Plan Colombia from a regional development initiative, as originally envisaged by Pastrana, to an aggressive military engagement with what were still characterized by the USA as the FARC 'narco-guerrillas'.

In total, Colombia was allocated $860 million under Plan Colombia (with Bolivia, Peru and Ecuador receiving the rest), of which 75 per cent was in the form of military aid. Through the provision of the money and the subsequent conditions attached to it, the USA significantly shifted the emphasis from rural development and civil society building to the militarization of Colombia's southern regions where the FARC were strongest due to their historical ties to the peasantry.[47] The principal funding for Plan Colombia was under the State Department's International Narcotics Control programme. Plan Colombia thus represented the most significant escalation of post-Cold War US commitment to Colombia in the form of a significantly escalated US militarization using the justification of a war on drugs. Contained within the Plan were three clearly articulated objectives: economic development, coca eradication and the improvement of human rights.[48]

The US government argued that a commitment to economic development was integral to Plan Colombia. Pastrana outlined the centrality of poverty in the explosion of violence and narco-trafficking in Colombia:

> Most of the program that we want to invest in the Plan Colombia wants to go really into implement policies on health, on structural reforms, strengthening our institutions, human rights and alternative development and social investment. We want to get into the real essence of the problem: that is, bringing back to Colombia prosperity and health and

richness to our people, and that's the way of eradicating drugs from our soil and from our territory.[49]

In 1998 the USA spent $750,000 on alternative development pro- grammes for the displaced peasants and coca growers in Colombia who had lost their main source of income through US-sponsored fumigation efforts. Under Plan Colombia the US government proposed $68.5 million for alternative development that took the form of 'community pacts'. These pacts were agreements between the Colombian government and those coca farmers whose total coca crop constituted three or fewer hectares. The USA stated that if these coca farmers would voluntarily eradicate their crops, the pacts would provide monetary and technical assistance with substitution crops such as maize, mango or coffee. By July 2001, in the Putumayo region, approximately 37,000 families had signed the pacts (the area most effected by the spraying of anti-coca herbicides). Additionally, $15 million of the economic development aid was to go to peasants who would inevitably be displaced as a direct result of the militarization of Colombia's southern regions. This money was in addition to $22.5 million allocated within Plan Colombia for the 1.5 million internally displaced people within Colombia's borders and constituted 20 per cent of the total of Plan Colombia.[50] Thomas Pickering, then US Under Secretary of State for Political Affairs, argued that this developmental aid was vital as it will 'counterbalance drug trafficking, in that it will help create alternative legal employment that will counteract against employment generated by drug trafficking as well as the same armed organizations that feed off it'. Pickering stated that the alleged success of the developmental schemes used in Bolivia and Peru where 'you can use the community to police the others to ensure that there's no return to coca cultivation' provided a model for US efforts in Colombia.[51] While the economic development aspects of Plan Colombia were a welcome addition for Colombia's civilians, a number of facts seriously refute Washington's claim to be promoting alternative development within Colombia.

The sum of $68.5 million for alternative development projects for Colombia was less than Bolivia's $85 million for fiscal year 2000. This is an uneven emphasis when we consider the escalation of military activity within Colombia and the subsequent refugee flows that have resulted from Plan Colombia's implementation.[52] The Washington Office on Latin America concluded that in 2001 a record number of 341,000 'people fled their homes ... making Colombia the world's fourth-largest host of internally displaced people, with over two million in a country of 40 million'.[53] Compounding this situation is the fact that, by April 2002, only 8,500 of the 37,000 families that had signed up for the pacts had received any money. Commenting on the social pacts, the Latin American Affairs chief at USAID, Adolfo Franco, told a US House sub-committee that it was a 'myth' to believe that 'large-scale assistance to provide new sources of income to 37,000 families can be identified, tested and delivered in one year'.[54] The Center for International Policy has argued that 'USAID is re-tooling its alternative-development effort in a way that, officials hope, will encourage coca-growers to move away from Putumayo, preferably to town centers',[55] with Under Secretary of State for Political Affairs Marc Grossman explaining that, '[i]f you can employ somebody outside of the county, and they will move there for a job, it's something that they ought to do'.[56]

The social and economic component of Plan Colombia thus closely resembles standard CI doctrine of displacing target populations consid-ered potentially pro-insurgency, and concentrating them in controllable (often urban) areas. The principal mechanism for civilian displacement has been the militarization of, and the insertion of paramilitary forces into, the conflict zones affected by Plan Colombia. The United Nations High Commissioner for Refugees (UNHCR) has shown that forced dis-placement increased by 100 per cent during the first half of 2002, com-pared to the same period in 2001, with the vast majority of the internally displaced forced to move due to paramilitary threats and violence.[57] The use of herbicides dropped from crop-dusting planes as part of Plan Colombia has also been effective in displacing communities. For example, the crop-dusting techniques have led to wide-scale food crop destruction throughout the regions affected by Plan Colombia. This in turn has led to large-scale civilian displacement and hunger, with Lesley Gill arguing that the use of herbicides on food crops 'raises disturbing questions both about Washington's commitment to alternative development and about the real aims of its fumigation program in guerrilla strongholds'.[58] This closely reflects aspects of standard CI doctrine highlighted in the previous chapter. For example, it is reminiscent of the call to relocate 'entire hamlets or villages [or] suspected individuals and families to unfamiliar neighborhoods' so as to isolate the people from potential insurgents.[59] Pastrana stated that the 'real essence of the problem is bringing back to Colombia prosperity and health and richness to our people'.[60] If poverty is the cause of drug cultivation, then it would make sense to put most of the money from Plan Colombia into developmental programmes, crop substitution schemes, land reform and so on. This would have a dual effect. First, displaced peasants who might otherwise join the paramilitaries or guerrilla groups would have jobs and thus incomes. Second, through the provision of economic development the economic grievances that often inflame insurgency would be lessened. However, only 20 per cent of the overall money allocated within Plan Colombia will be spent on socio-economic aid. The rest has been spent on advanced military hardware supplied by major US defence contractors. The original proposal put forward by Pastrana's government called for a 55 per cent military aid and a 45 per cent developmental aid split within the $1.3 billion plan. In the final US proposal, over 80 per cent of the money went to the Colombian military.[61] This US militarization of the Plan also weakened potential support of European countries that Colombia had originally hoped would contribute to the overall $7.5 billion funding package.[62]

The USA has also argued that Plan Colombia promotes human rights. There are two main ways in which human rights are allegedly factored into the Plan: the establishment of a secure environment and the Leahy Law on human rights monitoring. Clinton's Assistant Secretary of State of the Western Hemisphere Affairs Bureau, Peter F. Romero, argued that 'Colombia must re-establish authority over narcotics producing "sanctuaries". [A]ny comprehensive solution to Colombia's problems must include the reestablishment of government authority over these lawless areas. To achieve this, we propose to give the GOC [Government of Colombia] the air mobility to reach deep into these lawless zones and establish a secure environment for GOC officials and NGOs to extend basic services to these long deprived areas.'[63]

This is supposed to establish a secure environment for officials and non-governmental organizations to provide essential services as a prerequisite for encouraging economic growth and inward investment. General Charles Wilhelm, Commander-in-Chief of the USA's Southern Command, stated: 'While I share the widely held opinion that the ultimate solution to Colombia's internal problems lies in negotiations, I am convinced that success on the battlefield provides the leverage that is a precondition for meaningful and productive negotiations.'[64] The underlying rationale is the perception that rebel-held territory provides a safe haven for drugs production and the recruitment of cadres for the guerrilla movements. The pre-existence of the FARC zones of control requires a military solution both to extend the rule of law (and thus bring these areas under control) and to weaken the insurgents' power and bring them to the negotiating table.

The second supposed guarantee of human rights is the use of the Leahy Law whereby 'all assistance to the Colombian armed forces is contingent upon human rights screening. No assistance will be provided to any unit of the Colombian military for which there is credible evidence of serious human rights violations by its members.'[65] The USA argues that this will ensure that US equipment and training will not be directed towards any members of the Colombian military involved in gross human rights violations. Furthermore, a US–Colombian End Use Monitoring Agreement of August 1997 provided for the screening of unit members for past corruption. The agreement also requires Colombia's Defence Ministry to submit certification of ongoing investigations of alleged human rights abusers within Colombian military units every six months. In 1998 the USA refused assistance to three Colombian military units on the basis of their human rights record.[66]

Despite these arguments, the Colombian military has one of the worst human rights records in the Western hemisphere and has continued to maintain strong links with the paramilitaries throughout the post-Cold War period. Furthermore, there is a pervasive culture of impunity as a result of which members of the Colombian military shown to have committed human rights violations are rarely brought to justice.[67] Far from bringing security to what Romero calls 'lawless zones', the Colombian military has continued to bring lawlessness and murder to the peasant inhabitants of Colombia, as reported by international and Colombian human rights organizations.[68] As Plan Colombia's funding begins to flow there has been a corresponding increase in Colombian military human rights violations with an explosion of paramilitary violence.[69] Although the Leahy Law is intended to address the issue of military human rights abuse by refusing to supply, train or equip any army unit where collusion with paramilitaries can be proven to have taken place, there are dangerous weaknesses in the implementation of this law that effectively render it useless.

First, instead of vetting older units in the Colombian military for soldiers who have committed human rights violations, 'counter-narcotics' units are being formed from scratch. In this way, the emphasis in the Colombian military is on forming newly vetted units rather than investigating the 'bad apples' in the older units.

Second, a soldier from a disbanded unit can still receive training if his personal record is clean. He can then go back to his unit and pass on training. In effect this means that tainted soldiers within banned units can still receive training as long as they are not present initially when US military advisers are giving it.

Third, the Leahy Law relies on a large amount of transparency on the part of the USA. Every year the USA publishes the Foreign Military

Training Report (FMTR). The Center for International Policy regularly monitors the FMTR and publishes research findings based on its information. They have shown that between 1999 and 2002 the USA had increased the classification of information contained in the FMTR. This prevented 'all without classified access from monitoring implementation of the "Leahy Law" human rights restrictions' which had in reports prior to the increased classification shown that 'vetted individuals from Colombian Army brigades banned from receiving unit-level assistance were being trained' in direct contravention of the Leahy Law.[70] The classification of the FMTR thus made it 'impossible to oversee the US government's implementation of the Leahy Amendment' during the crucial period of US military aid escalation under Plan Colombia.[71] While the 2003 FMTR has eased the classification problems, it still fails to list the specific units in receipt of US funds and merely identifies recipients as Colombian 'police' or 'army' units. This is a crucial omission given the necessity of monitoring specific units in receipt of US funds and their past history. In short, due to the decreased transparency of the FMTR during the US military aid increase in the late 1990s, there was no way of knowing whether the illegal training of Colombian military units took place, while current reporting is not specific enough to allow effective and ongoing monitoring.

Fourth, while the Leahy Law encompasses most forms of military funding, the version of Leahy on Defense Department-funded aid, for example Section 1004, is much weaker than INC funding channels. Moreover, monitoring of Section 1004 funding does not apply to military exercises, arms sales and some forms of intelligence-sharing.[72]

Fifth, in implementing human rights vetting in Colombia, the USA solicits a list from the Colombian Defense Ministry of military personnel deemed to be free of human rights violations. However, in determining whether a potential trainee meets this criterion, the Colombian Defense Ministry checks both the Colombian court system and Colombia's Internal Affairs Agency. Importantly, this review ignores cases where credible evidence exists but has not yet resulted in any formal charges against the named individual. Human Rights Watch note that formal charges often take years to be filed under the Colombian judicial system largely because of underfunding and understaffing (which in itself gives an indication of institutional priorities).[73] When we couple this with the climate of fear that exists in Colombia and the frequent targeting of civilians who have accused Colombian military personnel of human rights abuses, this represents a serious weakness in US human rights monitoring in Colombia.

Lastly, the use of private contractors by Washington obscures legal oversight and end-use monitoring of training and arms. US mercenary companies like DynCorp Inc. and Military Professional Resources Inc. (MPRI) have provided logistical support and training to the Colombian military. These private contractors maintain databases of thousands of former US military and intelligence operatives who can be called upon for temporary assignment in the field.[74] This 'public–private partnership' is convenient in a number of ways. It allows Washington to deploy military know-how in pursuing strategic objectives while avoiding congressional caps on official military personnel overseas. Privately outsourced contractors also circumnavigate the potential negative media coverage of US military casualties, and thus lessen governmental exposure risks. Also, private contractors are accountable only to the company that employs them. Thus, if anyone is involved in actions that may generate negative publicity, Washington can plausibly deny responsibility. Myles Frechette, the former US ambassador to Colombia, outlined the utility of using private mercenaries when he argued that it is 'very handy to have an outfit not part of the US Armed Forces. Obviously, if anybody gets killed or whatever, you can say it's not a member of the armed forces.'[75] This private–public partnership thus seriously weakens the transparent operation of the Leahy Law, which covers only public money and the use of official US soldiers and equipment, and provides a high level of 'plausible deniability' for Washington.

In 2000, the Senate Appropriations Committee attempted to address some of these flaws by attaching six conditions to Plan Colombia. These included a more rigorous assessment of the prosecution of Colombian military personnel who are believed to have committed human rights violations, the prosecution of paramilitary groups, and the cooperation of the Colombian military with civilian authorities investigating human rights violations. A clause attached to these conditions, however, allowed the President to waive them if it was considered to be in the US national interest to do so. On 22 August 2000, Clinton signed a presidential waiver excluding the human rights considerations within Plan Colombia. The reason given for the waiver was the threat to US national security from drug trafficking.[76] Although Clinton maintained that he could certify Colombia on one of the seven conditions – that of bringing to the civil courts military personnel who have committed gross violations of human rights – a recent report disputes the effective implementation of even this basic safeguard. The report, prepared by Amnesty International, Human Rights Watch and the Washington Office on Latin America, argues that the Colombian government has 'been unwilling to take affirmative measures needed to address impunity, it has also worked to block legislation designed to implement measures that would ensure human rights violations are tried within the civilian court system'.[77] The areas outlined above represent a serious weakening of the intent of the Leahy Law and, as argued, the good intentions of the Leahy Law could see a lessening of emphasis on the bringing to justice of human rights abusers in the Colombian military in favour of forming US-friendly vetted units with little to no capacity of holding Colombian recipients of US military aid and training accountable due to US-imposed secrecy and outsourcing.

The use of the Colombian military as part of the USA's 'war on drugs' has been justified as a necessary response to the continued and deepening ties between the FARC insurgents concentrated in Colombia's south and international drug trafficking. Plan Colombia thus builds upon the earlier rationales given for the original Andean Initiative and US security assistance throughout the 1990s. The USA has argued that an aggressive supply-side destruction of coca plantations and military engagement with Colombia's 'narco-guerrillas' will form the primary component of Plan Colombia. The major US and Colombian military initiative under Plan Colombia has been the formation of two 950-man counter-narcotics divisions and additional funding for another division. The counter-narcotic units trained and equipped were said to be designed for a southern push into the Putumayo region of Colombia. The USA argued that this was where the majority of peasant coca cultivation took place and therefore where the counter-narcotic operations should concentrate. The FARC have long been active in this region, therefore the USA argued that the rebels have a vested interest in the coca trade and in protecting it from being destroyed. The strategic logic underpinning the US justification was thus the necessity for the counter-narcotic units to be highly trained and equipped to deal with potential clashes with rebel forces while undertaking their primary mission of drug interdiction and eradication activity. To this end the USA has continued to supply the Colombian military with advanced combat helicopters and has sent thirty more Blackhawk helicopters and thirty-three UH-1N helicopters to Colombian security forces. The sale of these helicopters represents the single largest arms sale to any Latin American country in the post Cold-War period.[78] The USA has also provided a $28 million upgrade to radar facilities in Colombia as well as sharing intelligence on guerrilla activity in the southern areas. A river interdiction programme will be deployed along the rivers on the Ecuadorian border to the south in conjunction with the recently upgraded A-37 aircraft used by the Colombian air force.[79] The US Department of Defense maintains that there are approximately 250–300 US military personnel and 400–500 private mercenary contractors in Colombia at any one time. These personnel act in an advisory role to the Colombian security apparatus. Typically these units are made up of US Special Forces and US Navy Seals or retired US military/intelligence operatives. In sum, the USA has continued to argue that the FARC narco-guerrillas make huge profits from the drug trade and use those profits to wage a war against the democratically elected Colombian government. Accordingly, under Plan Colombia the eradication of the coca fields comes first, and any engagement with the rebels is secondary and subordinate to the primary military objective of coca eradication. Central to the southern push against the FARC are the claims that the FARC are the biggest drug traffickers within Colombia.

In the south there is a pattern of small-scale coca cultivation by peasants displaced through the decades of civil war and unequal land-holding.[80] While this southern area hosts significant coca cultivation, it is by no means solely concentrated here. For example, in 2001 coca cultivation was relatively diversified throughout Colombia, with coca concentrations in eastern and western Colombia, as well as in the para-military strongholds in Colombia's northern departments.[81] Aside from the geographical areas where coca is grown, however, are the more important trafficking networks that are concentrated in the north of Colombia. These in turn are run, protected and sustained by Colombia's narco-mafia and their paramilitary armies. It is these trafficking networks that are responsible for trans-shipment into US markets and laundering efforts into both Colombian and international financial networks. It is fascinating that the USA has completely ignored these in Plan Colombia, and continued to insist both on its southern push against the FARC and that this push is driven by counter-narcotic concerns.

However, a report produced by the Council on Hemispheric Affairs found no evidence of the FARC's export of drugs to the USA. On the other hand, it did outline the extensive drug smuggling to the USA by 'right-wing paramilitary groups in collaboration with wealthy drug barons, the armed forces, key financial figures and senior government bureaucrats'.[82] More tellingly, however, James Milford, the former Deputy Administrator with the USA's central drug eradication body, the Drug Enforcement Administration (DEA), argued that Carlos Castano, who heads the paramilitary umbrella group the AUC (United Self-Defence Forces of Colombia), is a 'major cocaine trafficker in his own right' and has close links to the North Valle drug syndicate which is 'among the most powerful drug trafficking groups in Colombia'.[83] Donnie Marshall, the former administrator of the DEA, confirmed that right-wing para-military groups 'raise funds through extortion, or by protecting labora-tory operations in northern and central Colombia. The Carlos Castano organization and possibly other paramilitary groups appear to be directly involved in processing cocaine. At least one of these paramilitary groups appears to be involved in exporting cocaine from Colombia.'[84]

Unlike the AUC, the FARC operate a taxation system on the coca trade. This taxation system, rather than drug cultivation, trafficking and trans-shipment, was confirmed by the DEA. Milford argued: 'There is little to indicate the insurgent groups are trafficking in cocaine themselves, either by producing cocaine ... and selling it to Mexican syndicates, or by establishing their own distribution networks in the United States.'[85] Instead, he continued: 'The FARC controls certain areas of Colombia and the FARC in those regions generate revenue by "taxing" local drug related activities.' Nevertheless, 'at present, there is no corroborated information that the FARC is involved directly in the shipment of drugs from Colombia to international markets'. This view has been confirmed by the United Nations. Klaus Nyholm, the Director of the United Nations Drug Control Programme (UNDCP) argued that in 2000 the 'guerrillas are something different than the traffickers, the local fronts are quite autonomous. But in some areas, they're not involved at all. And in others, they actively tell the farmers not to grow coca.' In the rebels' former demilitarized zone, Nyholm stated, 'drug cultivation has not increased or decreased' once the 'FARC took control'.[86] Indeed, Nyholm pointed out that, in 1999, the FARC were cooperating with a $6 million UN project to replace coca crops with new forms of legal alternative development.[87] Nyholm confirmed this in 2003 when he argued that 'the paramilitary relation with drug trafficking undoubtedly is much more intimate' than the FARC's. He continued that '[m]any of the paramilitary bands started as the drug traffickers' hired guns. They are more autonomous now, but have maintained their close relations with the drug traffickers. In some of the coastal towns it can, in fact, sometimes be hard to tell whether a man is a paramilitary chief, a big coca planter, a cocaine lab owner, a rancher or a local politician. He may be all five things at a time.'[88] Nyholm's analysis thus confirms the DEA's analysis: namely, the guerrillas are involved in some aspects of the coca trade and raise funds through a generic taxation system. The Colombian government has also alleged that the FARC have traded cocaine for guns with Brazilian drug traffickers.[89] However, the FARC are 'bit part' players in comparison to the paramilitary networks and the cocaine barons that these paramilitaries protect. Both the USA's own agencies and the UN have consistently reported over a number of years that the paramilitaries are far more heavily involved than the FARC in drug cultivation, refinement and trans-shipment to the USA. Castano admitted as much when he stated that drug trafficking and drug traffickers financed 70 per cent of his organization's operations.[90] Instead of the term 'narco-guerrilla', a more suitable phrase would be 'narco-paramilitary'. However, this is a term conspicuous by its absence under Plan Colombia and the USA has continued to gear Colombian military strategy towards, and supply the arms exclusively for, an intensified CI campaign against the FARC and their alleged civilian sympathizers. In short, Plan Colombia's 'war on drugs' is actually a 'war on drugs' that some FARC fronts tax while side-stepping the paramilitaries' deep involvement in drug trafficking to US markets.

Why did the USA emphasize the FARC's alleged links to international drug trafficking under Plan Colombia and yet largely ignore the well documented role of the paramilitaries in the cultivation and trans-shipment of drugs? As we saw in the previous chapter, the USA was instrumental in setting up and institutionalizing a CI framework for the Colombian military that from its very inception developed and then incorporated paramilitary networks. While these networks were closely tied to the Colombian military, they have also historically aligned themselves with local sections of the Colombian ruling class, especially in Colombia's rural areas. For example, a number of paramilitary groups have acted as the private armies of large landholders, cattle ranchers and, during the 1980s, as the private militias of local criminal mafias intimately involved in the drug trade. Indeed, the US State Department has noted that although the 'AUC increasingly tried to depict itself as an autonomous organization with a political agenda', it was in practice 'a mercenary vigilante force, financed by criminal activities' and essentially remained 'the paid private' army of 'narcotics traffickers or large landowners'.[91] However, as with all armies, the narco-paramilitaries need funding for equipment, training, weaponry and so on.

The historical record shows that the USA has backed actors and organizations involved in drug trafficking so as to further strategic and/or political objectives such as CI campaigns.[92] The most notable instance of this in Latin America was during the US-backed Contra war in Nicaragua during the 1980s. In 1989, the Senate Subcommittee on Terrorism, Narcotics, and International Operations, the Kerry Committee, concluded a three-year investigation of Contra involvement with drugs by observing that 'one or another agency of the US government had information regarding the involvement [in drug smuggling] either while it was occurring, or immediately thereafter ... Senior US policy makers were not immune to the idea that drug money was a perfect solution to the Contras' funding problems.'[93] Given the evidence of the USA's clear knowledge of paramilitary involvement in drugs, it is apparent that it is willing to turn a blind eye to the paramilitaries' involvement as long as they cooperate with the wider US objective of CI. Indeed, the most visible success for the USA's attempts to stop international narcotics trafficking in Colombia was the killing of the leader of the Medellin drug cartel, Pablo Escobar, who by the time of his death in 1993 was one of the richest cocaine barons in history. His assassination was carried out by a group comprised of elite Colombian soldiers called the 'Search Bloc' who in turn were aided by the US Army's elite 'Delta Force' and DEA, CIA, FBI and National Security Agency operatives. Evidence has recently emerged that the Search Bloc were intimately involved with a paramilitary organization called 'The People Persecuted by Pablo Escobar' (Los Pepes) that carried out a wide-scale assassination campaign. Los Pepes was in turn linked to the Cali cartel, Colombia's second largest drug cartel after Escobar's Medellin cartel. Los Pepes was headed by Carlos Castano who later took charge of the national paramilitary organization, the AUC.[94] The CIA has refused to disclose any information in relation to alleged collaboration between US operatives and Los Pepes. This has led Amnesty International to file a lawsuit against the CIA in an effort to obtain all records which mention or relate to US involvement with Los Pepes. Amnesty have maintained that 'the CIA has improperly withheld these documents, which could prove ties between the CIA and notorious paramilitary leaders Fidel and Carlos Castaño, known to have worked for Los Pepes'. Furthermore, Andrew Miller, Amnesty's Acting Advocacy Director for Latin America, concluded that there was an 'extremely suspect relationship between the US government and the Castaño family – at a time when the US government was well aware of that family's involvement in paramilitary violence and narcotics trafficking'.[95]

In sum, drug trafficking provides a convenient form of funding for the paramilitaries and even in the highest-profile success of the USA's so-called 'war on drugs' in Colombia, the USA is alleged to have worked with paramilitary networks intimately involved with the drug trade. More ominously, the leader of Los Pepes, Carlos Castano, then went on to form and lead the largest and most powerful paramilitary organization in Colombia that continues to play a principal role in Colombia's trans-shipment of drugs into US and European markets, as well as committing the vast majority of human rights abuses within Colombia today as part of a pervasive campaign of US-backed state terrorism.[96] Meanwhile, the USA has refused to disclose potential CIA involvement with the Los Pepes paramilitary organization, or indeed the Cali drug cartel from which Los Pepes operatives were drawn. It has also failed to target paramilitary networks as part of its Plan Colombia, which its own agencies state categorically are the biggest drug traffickers in Colombia today.

From narco-guerrillas to narco-terrorists: the Andean Regional Initiative and the USA's new 'war on terror'

With the election of George W. Bush, the new US administration sought to lower the amount of military aid going to Colombia by 24 per cent. Accompanying this decrease for Colombia was an almost exact match in increases for the countries surrounding Colombia.[97] This new package was named the Andean Regional Initiative (ARI), and continued to be justified as part of the USA's war on drugs. The US State Department's justification for the 2002 budget argued that the goal of the USA in Colombia was to continue to 'help the Government of Colombia (GOC) to eliminate all illicit cultivation and the infrastructure which supports production of illicit drugs'. These goals were to be 'integrated into and supportive of Plan Colombia, the Colombian Government's comprehensive national strategy'.[98] In total, the 2002 ARI sent $367 million in military aid and $147 million in social and economic aid to Colombia. The bulk of the military aid will be used to maintain equipment sent under Plan Colombia and to continue training Colombian military units while the economic and social aid will be used for the programmes set up under Plan Colombia; 71 per cent of the total aid will go to Colombia's armed forces.[99] The 2002 ARI request also increased the number of US mercenary forces permitted in Colombia from the 300 figure in Plan Colombia to 400, while lowering the number of US military advisers allowed under Plan Colombia from 500 to 400. So far there are no limits on the use of non-American citizens.

In the aftermath of September 11, however, an explicit counter-terror orientation has developed within US policy. The primary means for the war on terror in Colombia has been the continued substantial funding of the Colombian military and a shift from the language of counter-narcotics to that of counter-terrorism. US Senator John McCain argued that 'American policy has dispensed with the illusion that the Colombian government is fighting two separate wars, one against drug trafficking and another against domestic terrorists'. Tellingly, he continued that the USA has now abandoned 'any fictional distinctions between counter-narcotic and counter-insurgency operations'.[100] Thus, in the aftermath of September 11 the USA has dropped the pretence that its military assistance has been driven *solely* by counter-narcotics concerns and has started overtly to couch its funding in terms of a strategy of counter-terrorism targeted at the FARC, who are now being linked to international terrorism as well as drug trafficking. For example, US Attorney General John Ashcroft designated the FARC the 'most dangerous international terrorist group based in the Western Hemisphere'.[101] The US Assistant Secretary of State for Western Hemisphere Affairs, Otto Reich, argued that the '40 million people of Colombia deserve freedom from terror and an opportunity to participate fully in the new democratic community of American states. It is in our self-interest to see that they get it.'[102] Secretary of State Colin Powell has compared the FARC to Al-Qaeda by arguing that there is no 'difficulty in identifying [Bin Laden] as a terrorist, and getting everybody to rally against him. Now, there are other organizations that probably meet a similar standard. The FARC in Colombia comes to mind.'[103] The Assistant Secretary of State, Rand Beers, even argued in a sworn statement that it 'is believed that FARC terrorists have received training in Al Qaeda terrorist camps in Afghanistan', although Beers was later forced to admit that this was a lie.[104] Importantly, however, this more publicly acknowledged role of the USA in fighting Colombia's insurgents is popularly depicted as military aid and training for a pro-US democracy so as to suppress armed 'terrorists'. Missing from this understanding is any notion of the actual strategy employed, for example covert reliance on paramilitary networks, and the practices of state terror inherent within US-backed CI.

In augmenting this new counter-terrorist orientation, the Bush administration sent an emergency Supplemental Appropriations request to the US Congress for $28 billion for its global counter-terrorism policy in March 2002. Contained within this request were a number of provisions relating to Colombia that proposed that US military aid should now be used not only to wage a war on drugs but also to fight 'terrorist organizations such as the Revolutionary Armed Forces of Colombia (FARC), the National Liberation Army (ELN), and the United Self-Defense Forces of Colombia (AUC)'.[105] This shift in emphasis has continued with the Bush administration's 2003 aid package for the Colombian military (still named the Andean Regional Initiative) which allocated approximately $538 million for the funding year 2003. The 2003 ARI package also contains almost identical human rights conditions to those found in Plan Colombia but has softened some of the language used to monitor Colombian military collaboration with paramilitary forces. For example, whereas Plan Colombia specified that the Colombian military must be 'vigorously prosecuting in the civilian courts' paramilitary leaders and their military collaborators, the ARI calls for 'effective measures to sever links' between the armed forces and the paramilitaries. Similarly, Colombian military efforts at 'cooperating fully' with ending collusion now merely call for 'cooperation'.[106] The ARI has thus maintained the high levels of US funding for the Colombian military while decreasing the requirements on Colombia to comply with basic safeguards on human rights.

The ARI also contains a component that will send $98 million to a new Colombian military unit trained to protect the 500-mile-long Caño Limón pipeline owned by the US multinational oil corporation, Occidental Petroleum. This money will be used to train approximately 4,000 Colombian military personnel, and has been overtly couched in terms of counter-insurgency training (in addition to an initial $6 million for a 'pipeline protection' brigade sent in the 2002 appropriations request). The pipeline money forms part of the overall $538 million contained within the 2003 ARI. Originally, the pipeline money was to be sent outside the ARI and was instead to go through FMF channels. The logic underpinning this decision was that publicly the USA wished to maintain a strict separation between its counter-drug assistance sent under the ARI and outright CI assistance sent under FMF which is generally considered to be all-purpose, non-drug military aid. However, due to US concerns about Colombia's delayed signing of an Article 98 agreement which exempts US personnel from being prosecuted by the International Criminal Court for possible human rights violations, the money ended up being sent under the ARI anyway, which is unaffected by Article 98 considerations. This further underscores the interchangeability of alleged US counter-drug assistance (ARI) and US CI assistance (FMF) which is supposedly technically separate. US ambassador to Colombia Anne Patterson stated that the pipeline 'lost $500 million in revenue because of attacks' in 2001. In response, 'US Special Forces' have been training Colombian CI units along the pipeline. The $98 million contained with the ARI will allow Colombia to 'purchase helicopters' and the USA to 'continue training' the Colombian military.[107] The money will concentrate on training troops to clear rebels from the oil-rich Arauca region near the north-eastern border with Venezuela.

Alongside the pipeline protection unit has been the long overdue designation of the AUC as a terrorist group when it was included on the US State Department's list of Foreign Terrorist Organizations (FTOs) in 2001.[108] US Attorney General John D. Ashcroft also issued drug trafficking indictments against three leaders of the Colombian paramilitaries in 2002, including Carlos Castano, and three members of the FARC.[109] Accompanying the blending of the drug war with a war on terror has been the election in May 2002 of Alvaro Uribe, a far-right independent candidate. Although only 38 per cent of Colombians voted in the elections and reports state that the paramilitaries engaged in widespread intimidation to force rural Colombians to vote for Uribe,[110] he has been welcomed by the Bush administration and is fully committed to implementing Bush's war against terror in Colombia. As part of this war, Uribe has committed himself to implementing a wide-ranging new security agenda called 'Democratic Security'. An early indication of the direction that Uribe's 'Democratic Security' would take was his declaration of a state of 'internal commotion' in August 2002 that allowed the Colombian state to prohibit public rallies and impose curfews and order searches without a court order. Fernando Londono, Colombian Interior and Justice Minister, stated: 'we all have to be aware that terror leads to extreme instability in Colombia. For this reason, the government has decided to declare a state of internal commotion.'[111] In September 2002, Uribe also attempted to pass his first military decree allowing for the creation of military 'Zones of Rehabilitation and Consolidation' in which direct military rule replaced existing local government and military authorities carried out arrests and searches without a warrant. Fortunately, the Colombian Constitutional Court declared the zones unconstitutional in November 2002.[112] Uribe is also pushing for tighter control of the Colombian media by seeking to pass laws which censor reporting on Colombian 'counter terrorist measures' and Colombian military activity. One of the 'anti-terrorism' bills seeks to hand down sentences of eight to twelve years in prison for anyone who publishes statistics considered 'counterproductive to the fight against terrorism', as well as the possible 'suspension' of the media outlet in question. These sanctions will apply to anybody who divulges 'reports that could hamper the effective implementation of military or police operations, endanger the lives of public forces personnel or private individuals', or commits other acts that undermine public order, 'while boosting the position or image of the enemy'.[113] Uribe's proposals are reminiscent of the earlier 'Plan Lazo' initiated in the 1960s, which sought to fully militarize large areas of Colombia's south in the name of anti-subversive CI warfare. Uribe is also in the process of setting up a civilian militia network that closely resembles the civilian paramilitary intelligence networks initiated under Plan Lazo whereby US CI doctrine specifies the necessity of 'an intelligence network in the community for the purpose of developing information about guerrillas in the area and to insure the prompt exposure of any undercover insurgent sympathizers in the community'.[114] The media censorship laws also mean that the reporting of human rights abuses will be harder, which again reflects standard US CI doctrine that advocates press censorship to prevent negative media portrayals of the overall CI effort.[115]

In sum, the major difference between Plan Colombia and the ARI has been the stated rationales of US intervention which have switched from a discourse of counter-drugs to a new discourse of both counter-drugs *and* counter-terrorism. Thus the post-September 11 environment has seen the escalation of the USA's publicly stated commitment to Colombia as part of its global 'war on terror'. Asa Hutchinson, the new director of the DEA, stated that the USA has 'demonstrated that drug traffickers and terrorists work out of the same jungle, they plan in the same cave, and they train in the same desert'.[116] However, while the USA has publicly declared its support for a new war on terrorism in Colombia, it has long acted to make the principal terrorists more effective as part of its continued CI campaign against the FARC and Colombian civil society. Thus the USA is not only not fighting a war on terror but it continues to be the principal supporter of Colombian state-sponsored terrorism. As such, the new US war *of* terror in Colombia performs the same function as the earlier war on drugs: it provides a propaganda pretext for the continuing militarization of Colombian society so as to destroy armed groups and progressive elements of civil society that are seen as a threat to US interests.

While the FARC are responsible for a number of human rights abuses such as kidnapping, murder of non-combatants and ecological damage, the US Department of State has consistently reported over a number of years that the paramilitaries are responsible for over 80 per cent of all recorded human rights abuses in Colombia.[117] Alongside the increase in post-Cold War US military assistance to the Colombian military and the legitimacy that derives from it, there has occurred a massive increase in levels of civilian displacement and paramilitary violence.[118] Amnesty International has documented the long-standing collusion between paramilitary forces and the Colombian military whereby in 'areas of long-standing paramilitary activity, reliable and abundant information shows that the security forces continued to allow paramilitary operations with little or no evidence of actions taken to curtail such activity'. Actions taken by the Colombian government to combat paramilitary forces are non-existent despite claims to the contrary. Amnesty International continues that one Colombian military unit set up specifically to deal with paramilitarism was no more than a 'paper tiger', with the official Colombian government office that allegedly monitors paramilitary massacres 'a public relations mouthpiece for the government'.[119]

As outlined above, the US Department of State must certify to the US Congress that Colombia has met the human rights conditions attached to US military funding. For the 2002 aid package, the State Department certified Colombia on all three of its conditions and released the aid. The three conditions were the suspension of Colombian military personnel who can be shown to have colluded with the paramilitaries, the prosecution in civilian courts of members of the Colombian military who have committed human rights abuses, and clear and effective measures undertaken by the Colombian military to sever links with paramilitary forces.[120] US State Department spokesman Richard Boucher declared: 'The Secretary made the decision to certify based on the Department's discussions with the Government of Colombia and Colombia's Armed Forces, a wide range of international and Colombian non-governmental organizations active on human rights issues, and information provided by our Embassy in Bogotá' with human rights 'central to our policy in Colombia'.[121] However, the main human rights organizations that were consulted included Amnesty International, Human Rights Watch and the Washington Office on Latin America. They released a joint declaration after the USA's certification of the Colombian armed forces and argued that on every point the Colombian government has failed to satisfy the conditions laid down. Despite the certification, the Colombian government has failed to suspend 'security force officers against whom there is credible evidence of human rights abuse or support for paramilitary groups' nor have 'the Colombian Armed Forces demonstrated that they are cooperating with civilian prosecutors and judicial authorities in prosecuting and punishing in civilian courts ... members of the Colombian Armed Forces ... who have been credibly alleged to have committed gross violations of human rights'. Lastly, the Colombian government and its armed forces have not 'taken effective measures to sever all links at the command, battalion, and brigade levels, with paramilitary groups, and execute outstanding orders for capture for members of such groups'. In assessing Colombian compliance with the conditions laid down they used the 'benchmarks that were submitted as part of previous certification discussions with the State Department' and found that 'Colombia has made very little progress on meeting even these conditions, first discussed over one year ago'.[122] The director of the Washington Office on Latin America, Bill Spencer, stated that the 'decision to certify Colombia on human rights misrepresents the facts in order to keep the aid spigot open'.[123] The USA thus both ignores and misrepresents human rights abuses so as to continue funding the Colombian military for CI.

This is made clearer by the fact that in 1991 US DoD and CIA advisers travelled to Colombia to reshape the Colombian military intelligence networks. This restructuring was kept secret and again was supposedly designed to aid the Colombian military in their counter-narcotics efforts. However, Human Rights Watch obtained a copy of the order, which was confirmed as authentic by the then Colombian Defense Minister, Rafael Pardo. Nowhere within Order 200-05/91 is any mention made of drugs. Instead, the secret reorganization focused solely on combating what was called 'escalating terrorism by armed subversion' through the creation of what Human Rights Watch characterized as a 'secret network that relied on paramilitaries not only for intelligence, but to carry out murder'.[124] The reorganization solidified links between the Colombian military and paramilitary networks and further entrenched the covert nature of para-military networks with all 'written material' to be 'removed' and any 'open contacts and interaction with military installations' to be avoided by paramilitaries. The handling of the networks was to be conducted covertly which allowed for the 'necessary flexibility to cover targets of interest'. Once the reorganization was complete, paramilitary violence 'dramatically increased' in Colombia, with the victims primarily trade unionists, journalists, teachers, human rights workers and the poor.[125] Thus, the USA further incorporated the principal terrorist networks into the prevailing Colombian CI strategy and sought to obscure further the links by making the relationship more covert.

The USA is thus in the position of having long worked privately to cement further Colombian military–paramilitary links on the one hand, while on the other publicly condemning the AUC and adding it to its own Foreign Terrorist Organizations (FTOs) list which carries legal sanctions. How do we explain this apparent discrepancy? The most plausible explanation is that the USA is facing a similar problem to the one it faced with Samper's alleged links to drug cartels: legitimacy. Castano has made no secret of his organization's deep involvement in drugs. When this is combined with the well-documented human rights abuses committed by the AUC, coupled with the increased international attention on Colombia and US policy as a result of Plan Colombia, there is an obvious crisis of legitimacy whereby the USA cannot be seen to be publicly condemning the FARC while continuing to ignore the paramilitaries. The most obvious example of this discrepancy was the long overdue designation of the AUC as a terrorist organization in 2001. In contrast, the FARC and ELN had been on the FTO list since 1997 despite the fact the AUC have long been responsible for the vast majority of human rights abuses against civilians. The harsher US rhetoric directed against the AUC serves to stem this legitimacy gap while the reality on the ground in Colombia points towards 'business as usual'. The recent internal developments in Colombia, and in particular the establishment of the new nationwide civilian militia network, will serve effectively to incorporate and recycle paramilitary networks into a formalized national security state structure predicated on a CI total war against the FARC and Colombian progressive civil society. For example, talks between Uribe's government and the AUC are ongoing, with Justice Minister Fernando Londono stating that both sides 'are working very sincerely'. A regional commander of the AUC declared, 'Uribe is like heaven compared to Pastrana'.[126] Gordon Sumner, former President Reagan's special envoy to Latin America, outlined the best way to incorporate the paramilitaries within the militia networks: 'First, have them answer the law, cut out the drugs, and embrace human rights', then try to 'bring them under the tent, to fight against the guerrillas, who are the biggest threat'. He went on to note that in Colombia the 'battle is never too crowded with friends'.[127] Uribe has commenced negotiations with the AUC (and has thus recognized them as a distinct political actor), and has put a bill before the Colombian Congress that will allow paramilitary leaders to buy themselves immunity from punishment for human rights abuses. This 'amnesty bill' essentially amounts to 'checkbook impunity', Human Rights Watch conclude,[128] while the UN has condemned the bill and argues that it 'opens the door to impunity' as it 'voids prison sentences by allowing responsible parties to avoid spending a single day in jail'.[129]

In essence, then, both the US and Colombian states publicly condemn the paramilitaries while privately relying on them to carry out murders, land clearances and 'political cleansing' operations. Meanwhile, a legal framework is being prepared that will serve to legalize the paramilitary networks. This is evident not only through the long history of US-backed CI in Colombia that from its inception relied on paramilitary forces, but also through the day-to-day unfolding of events on the ground. For example, the most recent military offensives at the time of writing frequently involved the taking of territory by conventional Colombian military personnel and then the insertion of paramilitary forces to hold and control the captured territory. In one instance, according to the UN, the military arrested 2,000 people in Colombia's oil-rich Arauca municipality. Only forty-nine of those arrested were brought before the courts, of whom twenty 'belonged to social or trade union organizations' while 'grave abuses by the Army were reported, including executions'. The UN continued that while the Colombian military intensified its CI operations 'paramilitary groups penetrated some places' and 'maintained their presence despite military operations'.[130] There are also reports that the offensive operations by US-trained troops in Arauca were not only designed to roll back the rebels in this oil-rich region, but also to secure a beachhead for further exploration by oil transnationals.[131] Meanwhile, Colin Powell has broadly supported Uribe's policies and argued that the USA is 'firmly committed to President Uribe and his new national security strategy', with the Bush administration working 'with our Congress to provide additional funding for Colombia'.[132]

In sum, throughout the post-Cold War period the USA has actively worked to strengthen the principal terrorist networks in Colombia while making this strengthening more covert and thus harder to trace. The Bush administration's 'war of terrorism' is reliant for its effectiveness on the Colombian military–paramilitary networks, which are now being legally incorporated into a national security state framework of CI state terrorism under the presidency of Uribe.

Both of the stated justifications for US post-Cold War policy are in fact pretexts used to maintain support for the Colombian military and, by extension, paramilitary violence. The war on drugs is actually part of a wider CI war against the FARC and Colombia's progressive social groups. This is clearly evidenced by the USA's misleading designation of the FARC as Colombia's principal drug traffickers and its use of the most powerful trafficking organizations (the paramilitaries) as part of its CI pacification programme. The counter-terrorist justification for US policy has even less purchase on reality with the principal terrorist networks in Colombia enjoying US support and supply throughout the post-Cold War period. The continued relevance of the paramilitary strategy is evidenced most clearly by the US reorganization of Colombian military intelligence in 1991 that further incorporated paramilitary networks within the overarching framework of CI state terrorism. In short, the USA is the largest sponsor of the principal drug-funded terrorist networks in Colombia.

A commonality among the vast majority of analysts of US intervention in Colombia is the belief that US planners are sincere in their public declarations of policy objectives. Concomitantly and equally prevalent is the belief that US policy has failed largely because the USA has not managed to decrease the amount of cocaine entering US markets or has failed to eradicate terrorism in Colombia. As this chapter has argued, however, once we move from the rhetoric of US planners and the predominant framing of the issues, US policy has in fact been remarkably effective: it has continued to destroy alternatives to US-led neo-liberalism through CI while the prevailing framework employed to understand US policy has worked within the declarations of policy objectives laid out by US planners, namely counter-drugs and now counter-terrorism. Why has the USA continued to employ CI in post-Cold War Colombia? The concluding chapter examines in detail how we can account for this continuity in what is commonly perceived to be a period of discontinuity in US policy and objectives in Colombia.

Notes

1 *Washington Post*, 3 December 2002. <http://www.washingtonpost.com/ac2/wp-dyn?pagename=article&node=&contentId=A1176-2002Dec2&notFound=true>

2 State Department draft report, *Cocaine: A Supply Side Strategy*, 15 June 1989. <http://www.gwu.edu/~nsarchiv/NSAEBB/NSAEBB69/part1.html>

3 George Bush quoted in Kenneth E. Sharpe, *The Military, the Drug War and Democracy in Latin America: What Would Clausewitz Tell Us*. Paper prepared for a conference on 'Warriors in Peacetime', Inter-American Defense College, 11–12 December 1992, p. 8.

4 George Bush quoted in Mark Bawden, *Killing Pablo* (London: Atlantic Books, 2001), p. 85.

5 See the National Security Archives, *Guerrillas, Drugs and Human Rights in U.S.–Colombia Policy, 1988–2002*, Electronic Briefing Book no. 69, 2002, for a series of interesting declassified documents outlining the evolution of US post-Cold War policy in Colombia.

6 Ibid.; *Washington Post*, 1 September 1989; on the reform of Colombia's economy in the late 1980s see *Colombia Journal*, 20 January 2003. <www.colombiajournal.org>

7 Garry Leach, 'Colombians Protest IMF-imposed Austerity Measures', *Colombia Journal*, 6 August 2000. <http://www.colombiajournal.org/colombia22.htm>

8 Nina M. Serafino, *Colombia: Summary and Tables on US Assistance, FY 1989–FY 2003*, US International Security Affairs, Foreign Affairs, Defense, and Trade Division, 2002, p. 2.

9 See Center for International Policy, '*Section 1004' and 'Section 124' Counter-Drug Assistance* <http://www.ciponline.org/facts/1004.htm> for more on Section 1004 funding. No data are available on Section 1004 funding prior to 1996. Until 2001 there was no reporting requirement for Section 1004 funds and the reporting requirements were tightened again in 2003. Private correspondence with Adam Isacson.

10 National Security Council, Interagency Working Group Draft, 'Strategy for Narcotics Control in the Andean Region', 30 June 1989. <http://www.gwu.edu/~nsarchiv/NSAEBB/NSAEBB69/col11.pdf>

11 National Security Council, National Security Directive 18, 'International Counternarcotics Strategy', 21 August 1989. <http://www.gwu.edu/~nsarchiv/NSAEBB/NSAEBB69/col13.pdf>

12 Richani, *Systems of Violence*, pp. 70–3.

13 Central Intelligence Agency, '*Narco-Insurgent Links in the Andes*', 29 July 1992. <http://www.gwu.edu/~nsarchiv/NSAEBB/NSAEBB69/col24.pdf>

14 Drug Enforcement Administration, Drug Intelligence Report, '*Insurgent Involvement in the Colombian Drug Trade*', June 1994. <http://www.gwu.edu/~nsarchiv/NSAEBB/NSAEBB69/col33.pdf>

15 *Newsweek*, 10 September 1990.

16 Peter Rydell and Susan Evering, *Controlling Cocaine*, prepared for the Office of National Drug Control Policy and the United States Army (California: RAND Corporation, 1994).

17 On US arms sales to Colombia see US Deputy for Financial Management Comptroller, DSCA (Facts Book), *Foreign Military Sales, Foreign Military Construction Sales and Military Assistance Facts*, 26 September 2002. <http://www.dsca.osd.mil/programs/Comptroller/2001_FACTS/default.htm> On the role of the Colombian National Police in both the war on drugs and the war on insurgency see Washington Office on Latin America, *The Colombian National Police, Human Rights and US Drug Policy* (Washington, DC: Washington Office on Latin America, 1993).

18 *New York Times*, 15 February 1996; see also Russell Crandall, 'Debating Plan Colombia', *Survival*, 44(2), 2002, pp. 187–8.

19 For more on the US certification process and the decertification of Colombia see Henry L. Hinton, *Statement of Henry L. Hinton, Assistant Comptroller General, National Security and International Affairs Division*, United States General Accounting Office, February 1998. <http://www.druglibrary.org/schaffer/GOVPUBS/gao/pdf3.pdf>

20 Russell Crandall, *Driven by Drugs*, p. 45.

21 Crandall, 'Debating Plan Colombia', pp. 187–8.

22 Foreign Military Financing provides grants or loans to countries that wish to purchase US weapons or training. See <http://www.ciponline.org/facts/fmf.htm> for more on this.

23 Federation of American Scientists, *Colombia Arm Sales Tables*, n.d. <http://www.fas.org/asmp/profiles/colombia.htm>

24 Barbara Larkin, Assistant Secretary of State for Legislative Affairs, 'Letter to Rep. Benjamin Gilman', Chairman, Committee on International Relations, House of Representatives, 2 August 1996 (Unclassified) <http://www.gwu.edu/~nsarchiv/NSAEBB/NSAEBB69/col49.pdf>

25 State Department Background Paper, *The Proposed Sale of UH-60 'Blackhawk' Helicopters to Colombia*, July 1996. <http://www.gwu.edu/~nsarchiv/NSAEBB/NSAEBB69/col47.pdf>

26 State Department, *Backgrounder, Blackhawk Helicopter Sale Request – Colombian Army*, July 1996, <http://www.gwu.edu/~nsarchiv/NSAEBB/NSAEBB69/col46.pdf> The final agreement reached between the USA and

Colombia for military assistance to the Colombian military can be found here at col56.

27 Kenneth H. Bacon, Assistant Secretary of Defense, United States Defense Department, *Public Affairs News Briefing*, 26 March 1998. <http://www.defenselink.mil/news/Mar1998/t03261998_t0326asd.html>

28 *Washington Post*, 12 July 1998. <http://www.washingtonpost.com/wp-srv/national/longterm/overseas/overseas1a.htm>

29 *Washington Post*, 13 July 1998 <http://www.washingtonpost.com/wp-srv/national/longterm/overseas/overseas2a.htm>

30 *Washington Post*, 12 July 1998. <http://www.washingtonpost.com/wp-srv/national/longterm/overseas/overseas1a.htm>

31 Interview conducted by author with Stan Goff, 26 June 2002. Goff trained Colombian counter-insurgency units in 1992 during the Andean Initiative.

32 GAO quote taken from Center for International Policy, *International Narcotics Control: Colombia*, n.d. <http://www.ciponline.org/facts/inlco99.htm>

33 Michael Evans, in National Security Archives, *Guerrillas, Drugs and Human Rights in U.S.–Colombia Policy, 1988–2002*, Electronic Briefing Book no. 69, 2002. <http://www.gwu.edu/~nsarchiv/NSAEBB/NSAEBB69/part3.html>

34 *Washington Post*, 27 December 1997. <http://www.mapinc.org/drugnews/v97/n725/a05.html?1166>

35 *Washington Post Foreign Service*, 18 February 1999. <http://www.mapinc.org/drugnews/v99/n182/a03.html>

36 *Washington Post*, 27 December 1997.

37 US Embassy Colombia cable, *EUM Agreement: Signed, Sealed, and Delivered*, 25 January 2000. <http://www.gwu.edu/~nsarchiv/NSAEBB/NSAEBB69/col66.pdf>

38 Barry McCaffrey, *Statement on US Support for Colombia*, Office of National Drug Control Policy, Washington, DC, 15 November 1999. <http://www.ciponline.org/colombia/00111502.htm>

39 *Washington Post*, 22 June 1998.

40 *New York Times*, 15 September 1999. <http://www.mapinc.org/drugnews/v99/n1011/a10.html>

41 *Reuters*, 6 August 1999. <http://www.mapinc.org/drugnews/v99/n813/a09.html>

42 *New York Times*, 10 August 1999.

43 *International Herald-Tribune*, 24 August 1999. <http://www.mapinc.org/drugnews/v99/n896/a08.html?1268>

44 Fact Sheet released by the US Bureau of Western Hemisphere Affairs, United States Support for Colombia, 28 March 2000; see also *Le Monde Diplomatique*, February 2000 <http://www.monde-diplomatique.fr/en/2000/02/11lemoine> for an analysis of Colombia's IMF-led privatization process which *Le Monde* argues is the 'biggest white collar hold-up in the country's history'.

45 *New York Times*, 10 August 1999.

46 *New York Times*, 15 October 2000. <http://www.commondreams.org/headlines/101500-01.htm>

47 Ingrid Vaicius and Adam Isacson, *Plan Colombia: The Debate in Congress*, April 2000 <http://www.ciponline.org/colombia/aid/ipr0800/1200ipr.htm> For the full text of the Plan see United States Institute of Peace Library, *Plan Colombia: Plan for Peace, Prosperity, and the Strengthening of the State.* <http://www.usip.org/library/pa/colombia/adddoc/plan_colombia_101999.html>

48 Ibid.

49 Andres Pastrana with Madeleine K. Albright, *Joint Press Availability*, US Department of State, Washington, DC, 11 April 2000. <http://secretary.state.gov/www/statements/2000/000411.html>

50 See Adam Isacson, *The Colombia Aid Package by the Numbers*, 5 July 2000 <http://www.ciponline.org/colombia/aid/aidcompare.htm> for the final breakdown of the various aid proposals.

51 Thomas R. Pickering, Under Secretary of State for Political Affairs, *On the Record Briefing*, 10 May 2000 <http://www.usinfo.state.gov/topical/global/drugs/pick.htm>

52 *San Francisco Chronicle*, 19 December 2000.

53 Washington Office on Latin America, *Colombia Monitor. Taking Stock: Plan Colombia's First Year*, March 2002. <http://www.wola.org/Colombia/monitor_may02.pdf>

54 Testimony of Adolfo A. Franco, Assistant Administrator, Bureau for Latin America and the Caribbean, before the House Appropriations Committee's Subcommittee on Foreign Operations, *U.S. Assistance to Colombia and the Andean Region*, 10 April 2002. <http://www.usaid.gov/press/spe_test/testimony/2002/ty020410.html>

55 Ingrid Vaicius and Adam Isacson, Center for International Policy, *The 'War on Drugs' Meets the 'War on Terror,'* February 2003. <http://www.ciponline.org/colombia/0302ipr.htm>

56 Marc Grossman, *Senate Foreign Relations Subcommittee on the Western Hemisphere*, transcript, 24 April 2002.

57 UNHCR statistics quoted by the Norwegian Refugee Council, *Displacement Increasingly Used as a Strategy of War According to UNCHR*, 2003. <http://www.db.idpproject.org/Sites/IdpProjectDb/idpSurvey.nsf/wViewCountries/9ACDAA14EE1D313EC1256BCD00572CDD>

58 See Lesley Gill, *Colombia: Unveiling U.S. Policy*, 19 April 2002. <http://www.fpif.org/commentary/2002/0204colombia_body.html>

59 US Department of the Army, *US Army Counterinsurgency Forces*, FM31-22, 1963, pp. 106–7.

60 Pastrana and Albright, *Joint Press Availability*.

61 For a breakdown of the various proposals for the military/social aid split in Plan Colombia see <http://www.ciponline.org/991001co.htm>

62 *New York Times*, 15 October 2000. <http://www.commondreams.org/headlines/101500-01.htm>

63 Peter F. Romero, *Statement before the House Subcommittee of Criminal Justice, Drug Policy, and Human Resources*, 15 February 2000. <http://www.state.gov/www.policy_remarks/2000/000215_romero_colombia.html>

64 Washington File, Press and Culture Section, *General Wilhelm Testifies on Proposed U.S. Aid to Colombia*, 15 February 2000. <http://ns.usembassy.ro/USIS/Washington-File/200/00-02-15/eur215.htm>

65 Bureau of Western Hemisphere Affairs, Fact Sheet, 28 March 2000.

66 Center for International Policy, *Colombia Country Overview.* <http://www.ciponline.org/facts/co.htm>

67 Giraldo, *Colombia*, pp. 66–74.

68 Joint Report prepared by Amnesty International, Human Rights Watch and the Washington Office on Latin America, *Colombia Certification*, n.d. <http://www.hrw.org/campaigns/colombia/certification.htm>

69 *El Espectador*, 19 March 2001.

70 Center for International Policy, *Training: Findings and Recommendations*, n.d. <http://www.ciponline.org/facts/traifind.htm>

71 Center for International Policy, *The Foreign Military Training Report*, n.d. <http://www.ciponline.org/facts/fmtr.htm>

72 Adam Isacson, Center for International Policy, private correspondence with author, 3 March 2003.

73 Human Rights Watch, *The 'Sixth Division': Military and Paramilitary Ties and US Policy in Colombia, Appendix Four, US Human Rights Vetting*, September 2001. <http://www.hrw.org/reports/2001/colombia/app4.htm>

74 *Dallas Morning News*, 27 February 2000. <http://www.colombiasupport.net/200002/dmn-contractors-0227.html>

75 Myles Frechette quoted in *St Petersburg Times*, 3 December 2002.

76 Richard Boucher, Press Statement, *Plan Colombia Certification Requirements*, 23 August 2000. <http://secretary.state.gov/www/briefings/statements/2000/ps000823.html>

77 Amnesty International, Human Rights Watch and the Washington Office on Latin America, *Colombia Certification*.

78 Federation of American Scientists (FAS), *Arms Transfers to Colombia: 1993 to Present May 2000.* <http://www.fas.org/asmp/profiles/colombia_armstable.htm>

79 Rand Beers, US Assistant Secretary for International Narcotics and Law Enforcement Affairs, *Remarks before the Western Hemisphere, Peace Corps, Narcotics and Terrorism Subcommittee*, Washington, DC, 25 February 2000. <http://www.state.gov/www/policy_remarks/2000/000225_beers_sfrc.html>

80 Isacson, *Getting in Deeper* (Washington, DC: Center for International Policy, 2002).

81 Vaicius and Isacson, Center for International Policy, *The 'War on Drugs' Meets the 'War on Terror'.*

82 Council on Hemispheric Affairs, *Drugs Replace Communism as the Point of Entry for US Policy on Latin America*, August 1999. <http://www.coha.org/PressReleases/99.14Colombia.html>

83 James Milford, *DEA Congressional Testimony*, House International Relations Committee, Subcommittee on the Western Hemisphere, 16 July 1997. <http://www.usdoj.gov/dea/pubs/cngrtest/ct970716.htm>

84 *DEA Congressional Testimony. Statement of Donnie R. Marshall*, Senate Caucus on International Narcotics Control, 28 February 2001. <http://www.usdoj.gov/dea/pubs/cngrtest/ct022801.htm>

85 Milford, *DEA Congressional Testimony*.

86 *Washington Post*, 10 April 2000.

87 *Associated Press*, 6 August 1999.

88 Correspondence conducted by author with Klaus Nyholm, 23 January 2003.

89 *El Rescate*, 22 April 2001.

90 *Reuters*, 6 September 2000.

91 State Department Human Rights Report, *Colombia: Country Reports on Human Rights Practices*, 2001. <http://www.state.gov/g/drl/rls/hrrpt/2001/wha/8326.htm>

92 For an overview of CIA involvement with drugs from the Second World War onwards see McCoy, *The Politics of Heroin*; see also Dale-Scott and Marshall, *Cocaine Politics* for an excellent overview of CIA involvement in the drug trade during the US-backed Contra war in Nicaragua. For an earlier study on the global trade in opium see Catherine Lamour and Michel R. Lamberti, *The Second Opium War* (London: Penguin Books, 1972).

93 Senate Committee on Foreign Relations, Subcommittee on Terrorism, Narcotics and International Operations, *Drugs, Law Enforcement and Foreign Policy*, June 1989. <http://ciadrugs.homestead.com/files/index.html>

94 For background see Mark Bowden, *Killing Pablo* (London: Atlantic Books, 2001).

95 Amnesty International, *Amnesty International USA Sues CIA for Information About Colombia's Notorious 'Pepes'*, 25 April 2001. <http://www.amnestyusa.org/news/2001/colombia04252001_2.html>

96 For background on Castano's career see Ana Carrigan, 'The Career of Carlos Castano: A Marriage of Drugs and Politics', in *Colombia: The Traffic of Terror*, August 2001. http://www.crimesofwar.org/colombia-mag/career.html>

97 See <http://www.state.gov/s/rpp/rls/iab/> for the State Department's Foreign Operations Aid Request.

98 International Narcotics and Law Enforcement, *FY 2002 Budget Justification*. Released by the Bureau for International Narcotics and Law Enforcement Affairs, May 2001.

99 See Center for International Policy, *The 2002 Aid Request*, 13 May 2001. <http://www.ciponline.org/colombia/2002request.htm>

100 John McCain, *Speech by Senator John McCain (R-Arizona)*, 6 June 2002. <http://www.ciponline.org/colombia/02060604.htm>

101 John Ashcroft, *Prepared Remarks of Attorney General John Ashcroft*, Drug Enforcement Administration, 19 March 2002. <http://www.ciponline.org/colombia/02031903.htm>

102 Otto Reich, *The Crucial Battle for Colombia*, US Department of State, 19 July 2002. <http://usinfo.state.gov/regional/ar/colombia/02071901.htm>

103 *Reuters*, 25 October 2001.

104 *United Press International*, 9 August 2002. <http://www.upi.com/view
.cfm?StoryID=20020807-123019-5992r> Beers later retracted the claim. See
Narconews, 'Beers "Corrects" Falsehood Under Oath in DynCorp Case'. <http:
//www.narconews.com/beersperjury1.html>

105 House Report, 107–593, *Making Supplemental Appropriations for Further
Recovery from and Response to Terrorist Attacks on the United States for the Fiscal
Year 2002*, p. 21. <http://thomas.loc.gov/cgi-bin/cpquery/R?cp107:FLD010:
@1(hr593)>

106 See Center for International Policy's *Relevant Excerpts from Conference Report on H.R. 2506, the Foreign Operations Appropriations Bill* for more detail. <http:
//www.ciponline.org/colombia/121901.htm>

107 Anne W. Patterson, *Remarks by Ambassador Anne W. Patterson at the CSIS
Conference*, Washington, DC, 8 October 2002. <http://usembassy.state.gov/
posts/co1/wwwsa034.shtml>

108 Office of the Coordinator for Counterterrorism, *2001 Report on Foreign
Terrorist Organizations*, 5 October 2001. <http://www.state.gov/s/ct/rls/rpt/
fto/2001/5258.htm>

109 *Washington Post*, 25 September 2002. <http://www.mapinc.org/
drugnews/v02/n1808/a10.html?1244>

110 *Common Dreams*, 31 May 2002. <http://www.commondreams.org/
views02/0531-07.htm>; Jeremy McDermott, BBC, *Profile: Alvaro Uribe Velez.*
<http://news.bbc.co.uk/1/hi/world/americas/1996976.stm> One of the
AUC's top leaders, Salvatore Mancuso, stated: 'A dignified President, Doctor
Alvaro Uribe Velez, has been elected conclusively and consciously in the first
round, by and for a Fatherland that wants to make itself peaceful and to grow
in solidarity.' Quoted in Justin Podur and Manuel Rozental, *Znet*, 'Prepare for 4
years of the Uribe Model Change and Continuity After Colombia's Elections'.
<http://www.zmag.org/content/Colombia/podur_rozental-uribemodel.cfm>

111 *AWSE News*, 13 August 2002. <http://news.awse.com/13-Aug-2002/
Politics/13233.htm>

112 *Colombia Report*, 9 December 2002.

113 *Inter Press Service*, 28 February 2003. <http://www.globalpolicy.org/wtc/
liberties/2003/0228colombia.htm>

114 US Department of the Army, *US Army Counterinsurgency Forces*, FM31-22,
1963, p. 99.

115 For example, part of US counter-insurgency doctrine calls for media
censorship. See ibid., pp. 106–7.

116 *News 24*, 7 November 2002. <http://www.news24.com/News24/World/
0,1113,2-10_1281687,00.html>

117 See, for example, US Department of State, *Country Report: Colombia
1999*, 25 February 2000. <http://www.state.gov/www/global/human_
rights/1999_hrp_report/colombia.html> State Department Human Rights
Report, Colombia: *Country Reports on Human Rights Practices*, 2001. <http:
//www.state.gov/g/drl/rls/hrrpt/2001/wha/8326.htm>

118 See, for example, Human Rights Watch's most recent comprehensive report, *The 'Sixth Division': Military and Paramilitary Ties and US Policy in Colombia,*

September 2001. <http://www.hrw.org/reports/2001/colombia/app4.htm>

119 Amnesty International USA, *Human Rights and USA Military Aid to Colombia II*, January 2001. <http://web.amnesty.org/ai.nsf/Recent/AMR230042001!Open>

120 Richard L. Armitage, *Determination Related to Colombian Armed Forces Under Section 567(a) (1) of the Kenneth M. Ludden Foreign Operations, Export Financing, and Related Programs Appropriations*, 2002.

121 Richard Boucher, *Statement by Richard Boucher*, 1 May 2002. <http://www.state.gov/r/pa/prs/ps/2002/9891.htm>

122 Human Rights Watch, *Colombia Human Rights Certification III*, February 2002. <http://www.hrw.org/press/2002/02/colombia0205.htm>

123 Bill Spencer, *Human Rights Groups Criticize State Department's Certification of Colombia*, May 2002. <http://www.hrw.org/press/2002/05/colombia0501.htm>

124 Human Rights Watch/Americas Human Rights Watch Arms Project, *Colombia's Killer Networks: The Military–Paramilitary Partnership and the United States* (London: Human Rights Watch, 1996), pp. 28–9. In the same report Human Rights Watch have provided the original documents of the order in both Spanish and English. See pp. 105–50.

125 Ibid., pp. 30, 38–9.

126 *Washington Times*, 28 January 2003.

127 Ibid.

128 Human Rights Watch, *Colombia's Checkbook Impunity*, 22 September 2003. <http://hrw.org/backgrounder/americas/checkbook-impunity.htm>

129 UN High Commissioner for Human Rights, Bogotá Field Office, *Observaciones al Proyecto de Ley Estatutaria que trata sobre la reincorporacion de miembros de grupos armados* (Bogotá: UNHCHR, 2003).

130 United Nations Commission on Human Rights, *Report of the United Nations High Commissioner for Human Rights on the Human Rights Situation in Colombia*, 24 February 2003. <http://193.194.138.190/pdf/chr59/13AV.pdf>

131 *Christian Science Monitor*, 16 May 2004.

132 *New York Times*, 5 December 2002.

6 | Conclusion: counter-insurgency, capital and crude

As argued throughout this book, US intervention in Colombia sought to stabilize a given set of social, economic and political arrangements that were perceived to be in its best interests. The principal means for this stabilization continues to be the training and funding of the Colombian military to destroy the armed insurgents within Colombia's borders, and to pacify unarmed progressive social forces using paramilitary forces. During the Cold War this policy was justified as a necessary response to the bipolar conflict while during the post-Cold War era the discourses switched to a pretext of a war on drugs and terrorism. Importantly, stability was not defined as the best arrangement for the majority of Colombia's people – for example, inclusive democratic arrangements or land reform – but came to mean the best arrangement for insulating Colombia's political and economic system from popular pressures and to ensure the stability of the Colombian ruling class allied to the US imperial state. In effect then, the USA was promoting stability for the few, and instability for the rest.

In respect to the US pursuit of stability, William Robinson argues that this stabilization of specific political and economic relations has both a national and a transnational dimension:

> US foreign policy is aimed at assuring the stability of a given set of economic, social and political arrangements *within* each country in which the US intervenes, *and* in the international system as a whole. The stability of arrangements and relations which girder an international system in which the United States has enjoyed a dominant position is seen as essential to US interests, or 'national security'. When these arrangements are threatened US policy attempts to undercut the threat.[1]

Robinson's point in relation to the stabilization of both national arrangements and the international system succinctly captures the regionalized considerations of US planners when pursuing stability in Colombia. That is, US intervention in Colombia cannot be separated from a wider set of regional US economic, strategic and political considerations that transcend conventional juridical definitions of sovereignty. As I now go on to show, the interlocking ties between US and Colombian capital

have continued to necessitate the preservation of a stability geared towards the maintenance of a favourable investment climate, unhindered
market access and the repatriation of profit by transnational corporations. This interwoven nature of the political economy of US and Latin
American markets has been made clear by a number of US planners.
For example, General Peter Pace, the former Commander in Chief of
the USA's Southern Command (USSOUTHCOM), which is responsible
for implementing US security assistance programmes throughout Latin
America, argued that vital US national interests, which he defined as
'those of broad, over-riding importance to the survival, safety and vitality
of our nation', included the maintenance of a stability geared towards
the preservation of capitalist socio-economic relations and the continued
and unhindered access to Latin American markets by US transnationals
in the post-Cold War period. Pace explained that 'our trade within the
Americas represents approximately 46 percent of all US exports, and
we expect this percentage to increase in the future'. He went on to
explain that underlying US military intervention in Colombia was the
need to maintain a 'continued stability required for access to markets
in the USSOUTHCOM AOR [area of responsibility], which is critical to
the continued economic expansion and prosperity of the United States'.
US security assistance to the Colombian military was necessary as any
potential 'loss of our Caribbean and Latin American markets would
seriously damage the health of the US economy'.[2]

Similarly, the current Commander in Chief of USSOUTHCOM,
General James T. Hill, echoed Pace's earlier concerns when he stated
that the 'US conducts more than 360 billion dollars of annual trade with
Latin America and the Caribbean, nearly as much as with the entire
European Community'. These trade links would increase, and by the
year 2010 'trade with Latin America is expected to exceed that with the
European Economic Community and Japan combined'. Moreover, US-
led neo-liberalism will further cement the integration of Latin America
with US capital; 'these links will only grow as we progress toward the
President's vision of a Free Trade Agreement of the Americas'. General
Hill outlined the utility of US military training and aid with the USA's
'Southern Command's security cooperation activities' serving to expand
US 'influence, assure friends, and dissuade potential adversaries' while
promoting a market stability 'through training, equipping, and developing allied security force capabilities'. Importantly, Hill argued that
'Southern Command will play a crucial role in developing the kinds of
security forces that help provide the ability to govern throughout the
region, and particularly in Colombia'.[3] Both Hill and Pace thus make

clear that US security assistance, particularly to Colombia, serves to underwrite the US-led liberal international order through the preservation of market access for US transnationals (the principal agents of US capital in Colombia). The largest non-state threat to this form of neo-liberal stability in the South American region is the Colombian insurgency. Stability therefore requires the eradication of this threat. Marc Grossman, US Under Secretary of State for Political Affairs, explained the logic very clearly when he stated that the Colombian insurgents

> represent a danger to the $4.3 billion in direct U.S. investment in Colombia. They regularly attack U.S. interests, including the railway used by the Drummond Coal Mining facility and Occidental Petroleum's stake in the Caño Limón oil pipeline. Terrorist attacks on the Caño Limón pipeline also pose a threat to U.S. energy security. Colombia supplied 3% of U.S. oil imports in 2001, and possesses substantial potential oil and natural gas reserves.[4]

The preservation of US access to South American oil is a fundamental consideration underlying US intervention in Colombia. US oil consumption rose by 15 per cent between 1990 and 1999.[5] In charting US oil dependency, the *National Energy Report*, authored in 2001 by US Vice President Dick Cheney, predicted that US reliance on foreign oil would continue to increase in the future. The report argues that 'the share of US oil demand met by net imports is projected to increase from 52 percent in 2000 to 64 percent in 2020. By 2020, the oil for nearly two of every three gallons of our gasoline and heating oil could come from foreign countries.' Crucially, the report outlines the fact that the 'sources of this imported oil have changed considerably over the last thirty years, with more of our imports coming from the Western Hemisphere. Despite progress in diversifying our oil supplies over the past two decades, the US and global economies remain vulnerable to a major disruption of oil supplies.' Tellingly, the report then recommends that the USA should make 'energy security a priority of our trade and foreign policy ... The security of US energy supply is enhanced by several factors characterizing our diplomatic relationships ... These factors range from geographic proximity and free trade agreements to integrated pipeline networks, reciprocal energy-sector investments, shared security commitments, and, in all cases, long-term reliable supply relationships.'[6]

As the report makes clear, the USA has sought to diversify its strategic oil acquisition needs away from the Middle East, while calling for US energy security to become a priority of US foreign policy.[7] Colombia is now the USA's seventh largest oil supplier and has discovered vast oil reserves within its territory.[8] More importantly, however, the instability in Colombia threatens regional stability, and in particular that of Colombia's neighbour, Venezuela, one of the USA's *largest* suppliers of oil. Paul D. Coverdell, a Republican senator, explained the regional focus of US intervention in Colombia with the 'destabilization of Colombia' directly affecting 'bordering Venezuela, now generally regarded as our largest oil supplier. In fact, the oil picture in Latin America is strikingly similar to that of the Middle East, except that Colombia provides us more oil today than Kuwait did then. This crisis, like the one in Kuwait, threatens to spill over into many nations, all of which are allies.'[9] Peter Pace outlined the wider strategic considerations of US access to South American oil, and linked US intervention in Colombia to fears of regional instability generated by the FARC. He started by explaining how important South American oil is to the USA, arguing that there is a 'common misperception' that the USA 'is completely dependent on the Middle East' for oil, when in fact Venezuela provides '15%–19% of our imported oil in any given month'. Pace then went on to note that the 'internal conflict in Colombia poses a direct threat to regional stability' and US oil interests, with 'Venezuela, Ecuador, and Panama' the 'most vulnerable to destabilization due to Colombian insurgent activity along their borders'.[10] As argued, the political economy of US oil acquisition has been gradually diversifying from an over-reliance on Middle Eastern sources towards a greater dependence on South American oil. Insurgent activity within Colombia thus not only threatens the economic interests of US oil transnationals within Colombia itself, but also represents a strategic threat to the US economy (which is heavily dependent on South American oil) as it destabilizes the surrounding region both through conflict overspill, refugee flows and through their potential links to other insurgent forces in the region.

Unhindered access to South American oil has become an even more pressing concern for US planners after the September 11 attacks and the continuing instability generated by the Anglo-American occupation of Iraq. The US ambassador to Colombia, Anne Patterson, explained that 'after September 11, the issue of oil security has become a priority for the United States', especially as the 'traditional oil sources for the United States' in the Middle East have become even 'less secure'. By sourcing US energy needs from Colombia, which 'after Mexico and Venezuela' is 'the most important oil country in the region', the USA would have 'a small margin to work with' in the face of a crisis and could 'avoid [oil] price speculation'.[11] The centrality of US oil concerns in Colombia has been illustrated clearly with the Bush administration's request for $98 million for a specially trained Colombian military CI brigade as part of the ARI. Unlike the more generic Colombian CI brigades, this brigade will be devoted solely to protecting the US multinational Occidental Petroleum's 500-mile-long Caño Limón oil pipeline in Colombia.[12] US Secretary of State Colin Powell explained that the money will be used to 'train and equip two brigades of the Colombian armed forces to protect the pipeline' to prevent rebel attacks which are 'depriving us of a source of petroleum'.[13] Ambassador Patterson went on to explain that although this money was not provided under the pretext of a war on drugs, 'it is something that we must do' because it is 'important for the future of the country, for our oil sources and for the confidence of our investors'.[14]

This new security arrangement between the USA, Colombian CI brigades and US oil transnationals essentially makes official what has been a longstanding relationship. In December 1998, for example, US mercenaries working for the US security company Airscan (which has managed the protection of Occidental Petroleum's pipelines in Colombia since 1997) were involved in planning a Colombian military attack on an alleged FARC column near the community of Santa Domingo in Colombia's Arauca region. During the attack a Colombian air force helicopter dropped a bomb on the community; it killed seventeen civilians, including six children (no FARC rebels were killed).[15] In their testimony to Colombian investigators of the incident, the helicopter pilots stated that the operations were planned at Occidental's facilities.[16] Similarly, the European Parliament passed a resolution in 1998 condemning British Petroleum for financing paramilitaries in Colombia to protect its oil pipelines.[17] The special pipeline CI brigade will thus formalize this longstanding and intimate relationship, and will use the so-called 'counter-narcotics' brigades for the protection of US economic interests. Bush himself made this clear when he stated in 2003 that 'the budget will extend the reach of counter-narcotics brigades in southern Colombia while beginning training of new units to protect the country's economic lifeline, an oil pipeline. In 2001, Colombia was the source of about two percent of US oil imports, creating a mutual interest in protecting this economic asset.'[18] In sum, the USA continues to arm and train the Colombian military for a CI war so as to guarantee a relatively unhindered source of non-Middle Eastern oil. Alongside these economic and strategic interests, the CI discourse also continues to function.

The continued existence of the CI discourse also helps to explain the continuity of the US-backed CI war in contemporary Colombia, and in particular the reasons why so many civilians continue to be targeted by US-backed Colombian military and paramilitary forces. As outlined in previous chapters, the CI discourse was instrumental in militarizing the ideological relations between Latin American armed forces and parts of civil society. Subversion became intimately linked to progressive demands for social, economic and political change. Concomitantly, those organizations typically at the forefront of change – trade unions, non-governmental and community organizations, human rights workers, civic leaders and so on – became legitimate targets of state terror principally through the use of paramilitary forces so as to distance 'official' state policy from 'unofficial' state practices. As explored in the previous chapter, the US reorganization of Colombian military networks in 1991 under Order 200-05/91 further incorporated Colombia's paramilitary networks within the prevailing security architecture. This in turn represents the most significant *written* evidence for the continued efficacy of a CI strategy predicated upon clandestine state terrorism during the post-Cold War period. Implicit within this pervasive strategy has been the continued existence of the CI discourse, which has continued ideologically to construct social relations between the Colombian state and certain sections of civil society in particular ways. The evidence for this comes not only from the continuity of the targeting of progressive social forces by the Colombian state but also from the designation of these social forces as legitimate targets within official discourse itself.

For example, in 2002 General Carlos Ospina, Commander of the Colombian Army, drew an equation between criticism of the Colombian military human rights record and support for the FARC: 'there's a coincidence of what the FARC say and what these guys [the human rights groups] say. I'm not accusing anyone, but there's a nice coincidence.'[19] Similarly, his colleague, Brigadier General José Arturo Camelo, head of the Colombian Military Penal Justice division, delivered a speech in 2002 at a conference in Washington hosted by the US Army. In it he stated that human rights NGOs were carrying out a 'judicial war' against the military and denounced these organizations as 'friends of the subversives' and part of a strategy coordinated by the guerrillas.[20] Pedro Juan Moreno, Security and Intelligence Adviser to President Uribe, explicitly stated both that NGOs were legitimate targets of Colombian military intelligence and that they acted as front organizations for insurgent groups. Moreno argued that 'Intelligence also has to be carried out on NGOs, because they are the ones that have damaged this country … [S]ubversive groups also work with masks, they work sheltered in those organizations.'[21] Fernando Londoño, Uribe's Minister of Interior and Justice, even equated environmentalism with subversion and argued that there continued to exist an international communist conspiracy to undermine the Colombian military through environmental politics:

> Colombia is the victim of an international conspiracy in which environmentalists and communists participate. ... [T]his diabolical conspiracy is also carried out when members of the armed forces are brought to court without any proof or evidence ... [P]olitical scientists tell us that communism is dead, but the communists are not and they continue to have their views and their will to fracture contemporary society. Frequently they dress in green, so they are the Green parties ... they all come together to figure out where they are going to hit and they painfully hit the prestige and the livelihood of Colombians.[22]

Most telling, however, was a speech by Colombian President Uribe before senior members of Colombia's armed forces who were gathered for the inauguration of Colombia's new air force general, Edgar Lésmez. He argued that 'when terrorists start feeling weak, they immediately send their spokesmen to talk about human rights'. He distinguished between 'respectable' human rights groups (but notably failed to specify the criteria for respectability or identify which groups he had in mind) and other groups who were 'political agitators in the service of terrorism, cowards who wrap themselves in the banner of human rights, in order to win back for Colombian terrorism the space which the armed forces and the public have taken from it'.[23]

We see then a very clear continuity of a CI discourse at the level of the Colombian state that continues to equate subversion with broad swathes of democratic activity and civil society organizations. Alongside the continuity of this discourse has been the continuing repression directed towards those sectors deemed 'subversive'. For example, in 2002 over 8,000 political assassinations were committed in Colombia, with 80 per cent of these murders committed by paramilitary groups. Three out of four trade union activists murdered worldwide are killed by the Colombian paramilitaries (almost 370 between 2001 and 2002),[24] while 2.7 million civilians have been forcibly displaced from their homes. According to the UN, lecturers and teachers are 'among the workers most often affected by killings, threats and violence-related displacement'.[25] Paramilitary groups also regularly target human rights activists, indigenous leaders and community activists.[26] The CI discourse thus continues to construct social relations between the Colombian state and civil society organizations in specific ways. In particular, the CI discourse continues to function so as to justify repression directed against progressive sectors of Colombian society that are at the forefront of both resisting the imposition of US-led neo-liberal policy reforms, and raising awareness of the human rights implications of US-backed Colombian state terrorism.

During the Cold War there was a mixture of interests and considerations that drove US intervention in Colombia and, despite declarations to the contrary, these interests have remained largely unchanged. For example, US access to South American oil was a critical consideration at the very beginning of the USA's CI assistance in the early 1960s. Colombia was one of the largest markets in South America for US direct foreign investment, which by 1959 was already concentrated in the fossil fuel industry (the oil industry accounted for over 50 per cent of all US investment in Colombia by 1959).[27] Throughout the Cold War, US planners also consistently feared the instability generated by the existence of the FARC and the threat the insurgency posed to capitalist socio-economic relations in Colombia. For example, in 1959 the US State Department concluded that 'it would be difficult to make the finding of present Communist danger in the Colombian guerrilla situation'; however, 'the continuance of unsettled conditions in Colombia contributes to Communist objectives' and threatens the 'establishment of a pro-US, free enterprise democracy'.[28] In a candid statement that shows the symbolic threat that the insurgency posed to wider US interests, and in what could almost be a policy declaration in relation to contemporary US policy (albeit without the Cold War anti-communism), the US State Department declared in 1964 that 'one of our principal objectives [is] the elimination of the *potential* for subversive insurgency inherent in the continued existence of active bandit groups, guerilla bands, and communist dominated "enclaves" in Colombia's south'.[29] Similarly, in relation to US strategic interests, the US Assistant Secretary of Defense for Special Operations, Colonel Edward Lansdale, argued in 1960 for US CI assistance for the Colombian military so as to 'correct the situation of political insurrection' in Colombia: a 'place so vital to our own national security' because of its proximity to 'the [Panama] Canal Zone'.[30] Echoing Lansdale's declaration in 2000, Pace argued that the USA had an interest in eliminating the FARC as the USA needed to maintain its freedom of access to the Panama Canal: 'Of particular concern is continued unencumbered access to the Panama Canal – a strategic choke point and line of communication that, if closed, would have a serious impact on world trade.'[31]

In short, contemporary US interests and considerations underlying US policy in Colombia have remained remarkably similar. These continue to be the defence of pro-US 'free enterprise' capitalist democracies against internal threats; the continued maintenance of US access to

South American oil and markets; and the destruction of the actual and symbolic potential of countervailing social forces such as the Colombian insurgents or progressive reformists. Importantly, accompanying the continuity of these interests has been the continuity of the principal mechanism considered to be the best way of attaining these objectives: US-sponsored CI. Conversely, a major discontinuity has been the pretexts employed to justify the continued US funding of the Colombian military. As argued throughout this book, the pretexts have switched from Cold War anti-communism to a new 'war on drugs' and a 'war on terror' in the post-Cold War era. Why did the USA change the discourses and why employ these discourses in the first place?

First and most obviously, the end of the Cold War affected the ways in which foreign intervention on the part of the USA could be 'sold' to both its own domestic populace and to international public opinion. Prior to the ending of the Cold War, official US state propaganda agencies such as the US Office of Public Diplomacy (OPD) were set up to man-age public perceptions of US policy and to sell US intervention in Latin America to both domestic and international audiences.[32] They were par-ticularly concerned to produce consent for the Reagan administration's interventions in Central America against the El Salvadoran insurgents and the Sandinista government (FSLN) in Nicaragua.[33] Importantly, the OPD concluded that anti-communism was becoming an increasingly ineffective pretext to justify US intervention in Latin America prior to the ending of the Cold War.[34] One OPD memo argued that new propaganda themes needed to be developed so as to 'stress and exploit the negative characteristics of our adversaries'.[35] These themes were identified in a key OPD memo and give an important insight into the evolution of US propaganda themes and their development prior to the ending of the Cold War. The memo outlines a series of 'supporting perceptions' that needed to be stressed so as to ease the administration's goal of portraying aid to the Nicaraguan Contras as a 'vital national interest of the United States'. These supporting perceptions were that the 'FSLN is racist and represses human rights', the 'FSLN is involved in U.S. drug problem[s]' and 'the FSLN are linked to worldwide terrorism'. These themes were identified using public opinion surveys 'to see what turns Americans against the Sandinistas' and thus produce consent for US intervention.[36]

The internal documentation in relation to the OPD's propaganda themes gives a crucial insight into the instrumental nature of the evolu-tion of US strategy in relation to the popular portrayal of its interven-tions in Latin America. Interestingly, the Bush administration appointed

Otto Reich, the man in charge of the OPD throughout the 1980s, as its Assistant Secretary of State for Western Hemisphere Affairs in 2002. In relation to Colombia and the use of the war on drugs discourse as a pretext, John Waghelstein, a leading US CI specialist, explained the utility of stressing drugs to sell US intervention to appropriate audiences. He argued that it allows a 'melding in the American public's mind and in Congress of this connection [leading] to the necessary support to counter the guerrilla/narcotics terrorists in this hemisphere'. With the linkage between guerrillas and drugs, 'Congress would find it difficult to stand in the way of supporting our allies with the training, advice and security assistance necessary to do the job' of CI, while those 'church and academic groups' who have 'slavishly supported insurgency in Latin America' would 'find themselves on the wrong side of the moral issue'. Most importantly, the USA would 'have the unassailable moral position from which to launch a concerted offensive effort using Department of Defense (DOD) and non-DOD assets'.[37]

This narco-guerrilla discourse was also used by public relations firms employed by the Colombian state itself. Opinion polls conducted in 1987 found that 76 per cent of all Americans thought that the Colombian government was corrupt and an abuser of human rights and 80 per cent wanted sanctions imposed upon it. To counter this perception and to make it easier to receive US military aid, the Colombian state employed the services of one of America's largest PR companies, the Sawyer/Miller Group.[38] The PR specialists' job was to transform the perceptions of the Colombian state as a corrupt and brutal abuser of human rights into a staunch ally of the USA in its so-called 'war on drugs'. David Meszaros, the director of Sawyer/Miller's Colombia account, explained that 'the main mission is to educate the American media about Colombia, get good coverage, and nurture contacts with journalists, columnists, and think tanks. The message is that there are "bad" and "good" people in Colombia and that the government is the good guy.'[39] Presumably, the 'bad' people were the Colombian insurgents.

In fostering these perceptions the Sawyer/Miller Group conducted opinion poll surveys and focus group sessions to evaluate public opinion. In 1991 alone, Colombia gave over $3.1 million to an advertising campaign. The campaign placed newspaper ads and TV commercials aimed at American policy-makers in Washington. The ads all had a similar theme. They asked the American people to remember the bravery of the Colombian military, stressed that the Colombian military was engaged in a war against drugs, and attempted to change perceptions of Colombia from being a drug supplier to the USA as drug consumer.[40]

Measuring the efficacy of the campaign is hard due to the absence of opinion polling immediately after the cessation of the campaign itself. What is clear, however, is that US military aid has continued throughout the post-Cold War era, and popular perceptions of the Colombian state include the belief that it is now part of the USA's war on drugs and terror and that it is a 'victim' of narco-guerrilla terrorism. Thus public relations, and the management of popular perceptions of international policy, are crucial to provide the needed legitimacy to sell US intervention both to domestic and international audiences. The internal documentation of the 'narco-guerrilla' discourse points to its conscious and clear development as a way of convincing both US domestic and international audiences of the continued necessity for US intervention. This discourse – combined with the newly emergent counter-terror discourse – provides a two-for-one bonus for US planners. First, it frames US post-Cold War intervention as ethically correct while the targets of US intervention continued to be portrayed socially as beyond the pale and thus legitimate targets. Second, it continues to allow for a militarized US engagement as both drugs and terrorism are popularly portrayed as dire threats to US national security interests. In this way the drug war and terror war discourses allow for the continuity of US military funding to the Colombian military who are, in turn, funded and trained to defend core US interests.

Given the arguments presented in this book, what are the likely scenarios for the future of US–Colombian relations? Sadly, the picture is not a happy one. The Colombian state remains firmly wedded to the implementation of neo-liberal reforms to its economy, and the increasing militarization of social life under the pretext of a 'war on terror'. The economic reforms that continue to be implemented under the auspices of IMF structural adjustment are pushing more of Colombia's populace into poverty. In 1999, at the inception of Plan Colombia, the World Bank concluded that 'more than half of Colombians [were] living in poverty' while Colombia's economy is effectively going into reverse in terms of its distribution of incomes. The World Bank continued that 'the proportion of poor [has] returned to its 1988 level, after having declined by 20 percentage points between 1978 and 1995' with a recession in the mid-1990s adding to Colombia's woes and contributing to 'a rise in inequality, a decline in macroeconomic performance, and a doubling in unemployment'.[41] However, the picture is less bleak for Colombia's elites. In 1990 the ratio of income between the poorest and richest 10 per cent was 40:1. After a decade of economic restructuring this reached 80:1 in 2000.[42] Meanwhile, under Uribe, Colombia is undergoing further IMF-directed structural adjustment in the interests of transnational corporations. In the oil industry, for example, Uribe is lowering the royalties paid to Colombia by foreign oil companies and has effectively privatized the state-owned oil company, Ecopetrol. Uribe argued that this was necessary so as to make Colombia internationally 'competitive' and to prevent Colombia becoming a net importer of oil. What he failed to mention is that instead of Ecopetrol exporting oil itself, it now buys the oil from foreign transnationals at market rates and then 'exports' it. Meanwhile, Colombia's oil regions are becoming fully militarized, with the paramilitaries effectively running a number of towns. This model of what Uribe euphemistically terms 'Democratic Security' is being rolled out across Colombia as an integral part of the joint US–Colombia militarization programme.[43] Given the ongoing difficulties in maintaining its occupation of Iraq, there is every reason to assume that Colombia and Venezuela will become increasingly important to US oil needs leading to further militarization, with Uribe's Colombia increasingly acting as a base for destabilization directed against Hugo Chavez's Venezuela. Aside from the regular allegations by senior Colombian military officers that Chavez's government is linked to the FARC, there have been a number of Colombian paramilitary incursions into Venezuela, including an alleged recent attempt at another anti-Chavez coup backed by Colombian paramilitary fighters.[44] Amid these developments the Bush administration is looking to increase its support for the Colombian state by seeking to raise the number of US troops stationed there while maintaining the very high levels of military assistance.[45] There is no reason to assume that a Democratic administration under John Kerry would follow a different path given his wholehearted endorsement of Bush's 'war on terror' and his hard-line condemnation of Chavez as a dictator.[46] On the other hand, the FARC continue to remain a formidable military force in Colombia, with Uribe's security reforms failing to deal the guerrillas any significant military blow. As such the FARC are not yet at a point of weakness whereby they can be drawn in to a peace process which ends the war but leaves intact the economic and social structures that they claim they are struggling against.[47] In short, there is a deadlock between the CI strategy of the US-backed Colombian state and the guerrillas which, in the absence of any political process or redistributive economic reforms, continues to contribute to the suffering of Colombia's civilian population.

As part of the new 'war on terror', the Bush administration has committed itself to an increasingly unilateral and overtly militarized policy of imperial policing throughout the globe. By labelling movements 'terrorists', US planners have operationalized a new discourse which operates in similar ways to the earlier anti-communism of the Cold War era. Importantly, this policy of 'counter-terrorism' effectively translates into the support and endorsement for a global war of state terror to 'stabilize' friendly governments against social forces that threaten the interests of the US imperial state and its proxies, while cracking down on dissent both within the USA and abroad. Colombia's war is one piece of this wider geo-political jigsaw. One of the central ways in which activists can resist these processes is through exposing the gaps between the rhetoric and the reality of US policy. In so doing the legitimacy necessary for US interventions declines, and the costs for global violence are raised. As Leo Panitch and Sam Gindin pointedly observe: 'an American imperialism that is so blatantly imperialistic risks losing the very appearance of not being imperialist' that has 'historically made it plausible and attractive'.[48] The spaces for resistance to state violence and structural oppression are differentially distributed across the globe. It is up to those of us fortunate enough to live in societies not characterized by pervasive state terror to make sure that the costs of implementing imperial policies are raised in various ways and made as unattractive and implausible as possible while struggling for a more just and equitable world order. It is hoped that this book has made a small contribution to this ongoing project.

Notes

1 Robinson, *Promoting Polyarchy*, p. 17.

2 Peter Pace, *Advance Questions for Lieutenant General Peter Pace. Defense Reforms*, United States Senate Committee on Armed Services 2000. <http://www.senate.gov/~armed_services/statemnt/2000/000906pp.pdf>

3 James T. Hill, *Posture Statement*, US Southern Command, House Armed Services Committee, 12 March 2003. <http://www.house.gov/hasc/openingst atementsandpressreleases/108thcongress/03-03-12hill.html>

4 Marc Grossman, *Testimony of Ambassador Marc Grossman before the House Appropriations Committee's Subcommittee on Foreign Operations*, 10 April 2002. <http://www.ciponline.org/colombia/02041001.htm>

5 *Pacific News Service*, 4 April 2000. <http://www.pacificnews.org/jinn/stories/6.07/000404-colombia.html>

6 National Energy Policy Development Group, *National Energy Policy*, 21 May 2001, pp. 27, 130.

7 For an excellent overview of the relationship between resource acquisition and US foreign policy see Klare, *Resource Wars*.

8 Donald E. Schulz, *The United States and Latin America: Shaping an Elusive Future* (Carlisle, PA: Strategic Studies Institute, 2000), p. 3.

9 *Washington Post*, 10 April 2000.

10 Pace, *Advance Questions for Lieutenant General Peter Pace*.

11 *El Tiempo*, 10 February 2002. <http://www.amazonwatch.org/newsroom/mediaclips02/col/020210_col_et.html>

12 *Christian Science Monitor*, 5 March 2002.

13 House Appropriations Committee, *Secretary of State Colin Powell before the Foreign Operations Subcommittee*, 13 February 2002.

14 *El Tiempo*, 10 February 2002. It is not entirely clear what Patterson means by 'our investors'.

15 *Los Angeles Times*, 17 March 2002; see also Rainforest Action Network, 'Oxy's Cozy Relationship with Colombian Military Turns Fatal', 25 June 2001. <http://www.amazonwatch.org/newsroom/newsreleases01/june2501_oxy.html>

16 'U.S. Pressures Colombia Over Human Rights Violations', *Stratfor*, 15 January 2003. <http://www.stratfor.biz/Story.neo?storyId=209166>

17 Human Rights Watch, *Corporations and Human Rights*, n.d. <http://www.hrw.org/about/initiatives/corp.html>

18 George W. Bush, *President's Budget Message on Andean Counterdrug Initiative*, Washington, DC, US Department of State, 4 February 2002. <http://usinfo.state.gov/regional/ar/colombia/andean04.htm>

19 *UPI*, 28 January 2003.

20 Human Rights Watch, *Letter to President Álvaro Uribe Vélez* (Washington, DC: Human Rights Watch, 21 April 2003). <http://www.hrw.org/spanish/cartas/2003/uribe_defensores.html>

21 *El Espectador*, 24 November 2002. <http://www.elespectador.com/2002/20021124/opinion/nota7.htm> Translated from Spanish into English by Ingrid Vaicius, see <http://www.ciponline.org/colombia/03042301.htm>

22 *EcoNoticias*, 16 July 2002. <http://www.iepe.org/econoticias/072002/16072002latin_colombia.htm> Translated from Spanish into English by Ingrid Vaicius.

23 Uribe quoted in *Counterpunch*, 20 September 2003. <http://www.counterpunch.org/podur09202003.html>

24 International Confederation of Free Trade Unions, *Colombia: Annual Survey of Violations of Trade Union Rights*, 2003. <http://www.icftu.org/displaydocument.asp?Index=991217688&Language=EN>

25 UN High Commissioner for Human Rights, *Report 2000*, 8 February 2001.

26 State Department, *Human Rights Report 2000*, Colombia, 26 February 2001.

27 Randall, *Colombia and the United States*, p. 241.

28 Mr Rubottom, *Subject: President Lleras' Appeal for Aid in Suppressing Colombian Guerrilla Warfare Activities*, 21 July 1959. <http://www.icdc.com/~paulwolf/colombia/rubottom21jul1959a.jpg>

29 Robert W. Adams, *Memorandum to Mr Mann, Subject: Helicopters for Colombia*, 14 May 1964. <http://www.icdc.com/~paulwolf/colombia/lazoadams14may1964a.jpg>; my emphasis.

30 US Department of State, *Preliminary Report, Colombia Survey Team,* Colonel Lansdale, 23 February 1960. <http://www.icdc.com/~paulwolf/colombia/lansdale23feb1960a.jpg>

31 Pace, *Advance Questions for Lieutenant General Peter Pace.*

32 On the role of the Office of Public Diplomacy and its use to sell US intervention in Latin America see the excellent National Security Archive, *Public Diplomacy and Covert Propaganda: The Declassified Record of Ambassador Otto Reich.* <http://www.gwu.edu/~nsarchiv/NSAEBB/NSAEBB40/>

33 For more on US CI in El Salvador and a critique of the justifications used to 'sell' US intervention see my (2003) 'Countering the Soviet Threat? An Analysis of the Justifications for US Military Assistance to El Salvador from 1979–1992', *Cold War History,* 3(3), 2003, pp. 79–102.

34 For a detailed analysis of the OPD, and a critique of poststructuralist approaches in International Relations see my 'Gluing the Hats on: Power, Agency and Reagan's Office of Public Diplomacy' (forthcoming), *International Relations,* 2005.

35 *Public Diplomacy Strategy Paper,* May 1983, p. 11. National Security Archive, Public Diplomacy and Covert Propaganda: The Declassified Record of Ambassador Otto Reich. <http://www.gwu.edu/~nsarchiv/NSAEBB/NSAEBB40/>

36 *Public Diplomacy Action Plan: Support for the White House Educational Campaign.* 12 March 1985, pp. 1, 4. <http://www.gwu.edu/~ñsarchiv/NSAEBB/NSAEBB40/00934.pdf>

37 John Waghelstein, *Military Review,* February 1987.

38 Stauber and Rampton, *Toxic Sludge is Good for You,* pp. 143–8.

39 R. S. Zaharna and Juan Cristobal Villalobos, 'A Public Relations Tour of Embassy Row: The Latin Diplomatic Experience', *Public Relations Quarterly,* 45, 2000, pp. 33–7.

40 Stauber and Rampton, *Toxic Sludge is Good for You,* pp. 143–8.

41 Carlos Velez, *Colombia Poverty Report Volume 1,* World Bank, March 2002.

42 Mario Novelli, 'Globalizations, Social Movement Unionism and New Internationalisms: The Role of Strategic Learning in the Transformation of the Municipal Workers Union of EMCALI' (forthcoming), *Globalization, Education, Societies.*

43 *Colombia Journal,* 10 May 2004; see also BBC website, 6 May 2002. <http://news.bbc.co.uk/2/hi/americas/3683851.stm>

44 *Bloomberg,* 12 May 2004; see also BBC, 13 May 2004. <http://news.bbc.co.uk/2/hi/americas/3709609.stm>

45 Transcript, Hearing of the Senate Armed Services Committee: 'Fiscal Year 2005 National Defense Authorization Budget Request,' 1 April 2004.

46 *Business Wire,* 5 May 2004.

47 The best account of the role that peace processes have played in ending insurgencies while leaving intact highly unequal social and economic structures is Robinson's *Promoting Polyarchy.*

48 Panitch and Gindin, 'Global Capitalism and American Empire', p. 31.

Sources

Internet resources

Foreign Policy in Focus, a progressive think-tank: <http://www.fpif.org/>

National Security Archive declassified documentation on US policy in Colombia: <http://www.gwu.edu/~nsarchiv/NSAEBB/NSAEBB69/>

Znet. Good general coverage of US policy in Latin America: <http://www.zmag.org/>ZNET.htm>

Colombia Journal. Analysis from Colombia's frontlines: <http://www.colombiajournal.org/>

Paul Wolf, a superb collection of declassified documents from a Washington-based researcher. <http://www.icdc.com/~paulwolf/>

Human Rights Watch: <http://www.hrw.org/>

Amnesty International: <http://www.amnesty.org/>

Colombia Week. A good source for independent news and analysis: <http://www.colombiaweek.org/>

North American Congress on Latin America. Good analysis on US policy in Latin America. <http://www.nacla.org/>

Office of the United Nations High Commisioner for Human Rights: <http://www.unhchr.ch/>

US Department of State Human Rights Reports: <http://www.state.gov/g/drl/hr/>

Center for International Policy. Superb resource on Colombia: <http://www.ciponline.org>

Media Awareness Project. Good media resource: <http://www.mapinc.org/>

Federation of American Scientists. Good resource on security and military affairs: <http://www.fas.org/>

US Drug Enforcement Administration: <http://www.usdoj.gov/dea/>

Books/articles

Barrow, Clyde W., *Critical Theories of the State: Marxist, Neo-Marxist, Post-Marxist* (Madison, WI: University of Wisconsin Press, 1993).

Berquist, Charles, Ricardo Penaranda and Gonzalo Sanchez, *Violence in Colombia. The Contemporary Crisis in Historical Perspective* (Washington, DC: SR Books, 1992).

Brown, Cynthia (ed.), *With Friends Like These: The Americas Watch Report on Human Rights and US Policy In Latin America* (New York: Pantheon Books, 1985).

Brown, Michael E., Owen R. Cote, Sean M. Lynn-Jones, Steven E. Miller (eds),

America's Strategic Choices: An International Security Reader (Cambridge, MA: MIT Press, 1997).

Bushnell, David, *The Making of Modern Colombia. A Nation in Spite of Itself* (London: University of California Press, 1993).

Chomsky, Noam, *Year 501: The Conquest Continues* (Boston, MA: South End Press, 1993).

Chomsky, Noam and Edward Herman, *The Washington Connection and Third World Fascism* (Boston, MA: South End Press, 1979).

Cox, Michael, *US Foreign Policy After the Cold War: Superpower without a Mission* (London: Frances Pinter, 1995).

Cox, Michael, Takashi Inoguchi and G. John Ikenberry (eds), *American Democracy Promotion: Impulses, Strategies, and Impacts* (Oxford: Oxford University Press, 2000).

Crandall, Russell, *Driven by Drugs: US Policy Toward Colombia* (London: Lynne Rienner, 2002).

Dale-Scott, Peter and Jonathon Marshall, *Cocaine Politics: Drugs, Armies, and the CIA in Central America* (Berkeley, CA: University of California Press, 1992).

Drexler, Robert, *Colombia and the United States: Narcotics Traffic and a Failed Foreign Policy* (London: McFarland, 1997).

George, Alexander (ed.), *Western State Terrorism* (Cambridge: Polity Press, 1991).

Giraldo, Javier, S.J., *Colombia: The Genocidal Democracy* (Monroe, ME: Common Courage Press, 1996).

Gleijeses, Piero, *Shattered Hope: The Guatemalan Revolution and the United States, 1944–54* (Princeton, NJ: Princeton University Press, 1991).

Haig, Alexander M., *Caveat: Realism, Reagan and Foreign Policy* (New York: Macmillan, 1984).

Huggins, Martha K., *Political Policing: The United States and Latin America* (Durham, NC: Duke University Press, 1998).

Hunter, Allen (ed.), *Rethinking the Cold War* (Philadelphia, PA: Temple University Press, 1998).

Kennan, George, *Foreign Relations of the United States, 1948* (Washington, DC: General Printing Office, 1976).

Kirk, Robin, *More Terrible than Death. Massacres, Drugs, and America's War in Colombia* (New York: Public Affairs Press, 2003).

Kirkpatrick, Jeane J., *Dictatorships and Double Standards: Rationalism and Reason in Politics* (New York: American Enterprise Institute, 1982).

Klare, Michael, *Resource Wars: The New Landscape of Global Conflict* (New York: Owl Books, 2002).

Klare, Michael T. and Peter Kornbluh (eds), *Low Intensity Warfare* (New York: Random House, 1988).

Kolko, Gabriel, *The Politics of War: The World and United States Foreign Policy, 1943–1945* (New York: Pantheon, 1990).

Kolko, Joyce and Gabriel Kolko, *The Limits of Power* (New York: Harper and Row, 1972).

LaFeber, Walter, *America, Russia and the Cold War, 1945–1980* (New York: John Wiley, 1980).

— *Inevitable Revolutions: The United States in Central America* (New York: Norton, 1984).

Laffey, Mark and Tarak Barkawi (eds), *Democracy, Liberalism and War: Rethinking the Democratic Peace Debate* (Boulder, CO: Lynne Rienner, 2001).

Lamperti, John, *What are We Afraid of? An Assessment of the 'Communist Threat' in Central America* (Boston, MA: South End Press, 1988).

Leach, Garry M., *Killing Peace: Colombia's Conflict and the Failure of U.S. Intervention* (New York: Information Network of the Americas, 2002).

LeoGrande, William M., *Our Own Backyard: The United States in Central America, 1977–1992* (Chapel Hill, NC: University of North Carolina Press, 1998).

Livingstone, Grace, *Inside Colombia. Drugs, Democracy and War* (London: Latin American Bureau, 2003).

McClintock, Michael, *The American Connection: State Terror and Popular Resistance in El Salvador* (London: Zed Books, 1985).

— *Instruments of Statecraft: U.S. Guerrilla Warfare, Counterinsurgency and Counter-Terrorism* (New York: Pantheon Books, 1992).

McCoy, Alfred W., *The Politics of Heroin: CIA Complicity in the Global Drug Trade* (New York: Harper and Row, 1991).

Melrose, Dianna, *Nicaragua: The Threat of a Good Example?* (Oxford: Oxfam Public Affairs Unit, 1985).

Nelson-Pallmeyer, Jack, *School of Assassins* (New York: Orbis Books, 1997).

Novelli, Mario (2005) 'Globalizations, Social Movement Unionism and New Internationalisms: The Role of Strategic Learning in the Transformation of the Municipal Workers Union of EMCALI', forthcoming in *Globalization, Societies, Education.*

Panitch, Leo and Sam Gindin, 'Global Capitalism and American Empire', in *Socialist Register: The New Imperial Challenge* (London: Merlin Press, 2003).

Passage, David, *The United States and Colombia: Untying the Gordian Knot* (US Army War College, Strategic Studies Institute, 2000).

Patterson, Thomas G., *Meeting the Communist Threat* (Oxford: Oxford University Press, 1988).

Pearce, Jenny, *Colombia. Inside the Labyrinth* (London: Latin American Bureau, 1990).

Rabasa, Angel and Peter Chalk, *Colombian Labyrinth: The Synergy of Drugs and Insurgency and Its Implications for Regional Stability* (Washington, DC: Rand Inc, 2001).

Randall, Stephen J., *Colombia and the United States: Hegemony and Interdependence* (Athens, GA: University of Georgia Press, 1992).

Rempe, Dennis M., 'Guerrillas, Bandits, and Independent Republics: US Counter-insurgency Efforts in Colombia 1959–1965', *Small Wars and Insurgencies,* 6(3), 1995, pp. 304–27.

Richani, Nazih, *Systems of Violence: The Political Economy of War and Peace in Colombia* (New York: State University of New York Press, 2002).

Robinson, William, *Promoting Polyarchy: Globalization, US Intervention and Hegemony* (Cambridge: Cambridge University Press, 1996).

— *Transnational Conflicts: Central America, Social Change, and Globalization* (London: Verso, 2003).

— *A Theory of Global Capitalism. Production, Class, and State in a Transnational World* (Baltimore, MD: Johns Hopkins University Press, 2004).

Rostow, Walt W., *The Stages of Economic Growth* (Cambridge: Cambridge University Press, 1960).

Ruiz, Bert, *The Colombian Civil War* (North Carolina: McFarland, 2001).

Rupert, Mark and Hazel Smith (eds), *Historical Materialism and Globalization* (London: Routledge, 2002).

Schlesinger, Stephen and Stephen Kinzer, *Bitter Fruit: The Story of the American Coup in Guatemala* (Cambridge, MA: Harvard University Press, 1999).

Schmitz, David F., *Thank God They're on Our Side: The United States & Right-Wing Dictatorships, 1921–1965* (London: University of North Carolina Press, 1999).

Schoultz, Lars, *National Security and United States Policy Toward Latin America* (Princeton, NJ: Princeton University Press, 1987).

— *Beneath the United States: A History of US Policy Toward Latin America* (London: Harvard University Press, 1998).

Sluka, Jeffrey (ed.), *Death Squad: The Anthropology of State Terror* (Philadelphia, PA: University of Pennsylvania Press, 2000).

Stauber, John and Sheldon Rampton, *Toxic Sludge is Good for You: Lies, Damn Lies and the Public Relations Industry* (Monroe, ME: Common Courage Press, 1995).

Stokes, Doug, 'Better Lead than Bread? A Critical Analysis of the US's Plan Colombia', *Civil Wars*, 4(2), 2001, pp. 59–78.

— 'Debating Plan Colombia', *Survival*, 44(2), 2002, pp. 183–8.

— 'Countering the Soviet Threat? An Analysis of the Justifications for US Military Assistance to El Salvador from 1979–1992', *Cold War History*, 3(3), 2003, pp. 79–102.

— 'Why the End of the Cold War Doesn't Matter: The US War of Terror in Colombia', *Review of International Studies*, 29(4), 2003, pp. 569–85.

Weldes, Jutta, *Constructing National Interests: The United States and the Cuban Missile Crisis* (Minneapolis, MN: University of Minnesota Press, 1999).

Williams, William Appleman, *History as a Way of Learning* (New York: Norton, 1988).

— *The Tragedy of American Diplomacy* (New York: Norton, 1988).

Index